Scrapbooking Student Writing

A Creative Way to Motivate Student Writers

by Paula J. Hyman

Carson-Dellosa Publishing Company, Inc.

Greensboro, North Carolina

Dedication
To my family—the most important part of my scrapbooks

Credits

Editor: Ashley Anderson

Layout Design: Van Harris

Inside Illustrations: Bill Neville & George Ling

Inside Sample Pages: Van Harris & Lori Jackson

Cover Design: Peggy Jackson

Photos: © 2001 Brand X Pictures

© Comstock, Inc.

© Photodisc

Table of Contents

Introduction

Teachers are always looking for new, creative ways to motivate student writers. *Scrapbooking Student Writing* provides that creative outlet. By the end of the school year, each student will have a personalized scrapbook that chronicles events of the year and displays writing progress. This book contains instructions and tips for assembling more than 30 scrapbook pages—each centered around a writing assignment! In fact, each project includes two writing options, and the writing assignments cover a variety of types of writing, including journaling, dialogue, lists, paragraphs, letters, fiction, nonfiction, and more.

Students who are emerging writers or students who are learning to enhance their written communication skills will enjoy showcasing their writing in artfully arranged scrapbooks. A completed scrapbook will not only be a wonderful keepsake for each student, it will also serve as a writing portfolio because it will be a written record of the student's writing progress throughout the year.

Scrapbooking Student Writing makes scrapbooking easy for you and your students, even if you have no previous scrapbooking experience. Using just clip art, paper, markers, and glue, students will be proudly creating pages to exhibit their writing. Enjoy the creative adventure!

  Scrapbooking Student Writing ✳ CD-104163

What's in This Book?

Worried that you've never scrapbooked before? Don't be! Even if you've never created a scrapbook page, this easy-to-use book will successfully guide you and your students through the process. Scrapbook pages can be as plain or fancy as the creator wants them to be. Tips are provided for simple decorations and lettering techniques (pages 15–17) if you or your students would like to add a special touch to some of the scrapbook pages, but you are not "required" to use them. As an added bonus, you will find reproducible pages throughout this book to use to create your own patterned background papers. Instructions for using these pages are on page 15.

The scrapbook projects in this book are organized sequentially from September through May. There are pages for summarizing each month of the school year followed by pages for major events, important days, vacations, etc., that occur during the year. Each project includes a full-color, sample assembled page(s), a materials list, instructions for assembly, teacher tips, black and white clip art for students to color, and two writing assignment options.

The two writing options vary in difficulty. Option 1 is an easier assignment that is best suited for reluctant or emerging writers. Option 2 requires more paragraph writing and allows writers to create longer stories or descriptions.

Finally, since organization is an important part of every classroom, the pages of this book are perforated so that you can tear them out. This will make it easier for you to copy clip art pages and display the sample assembled pages. When you select a new scrapbooking project, tear out the appropriate pages. After you are finished using them, store them in a file folder, notebook with page protectors, or large envelope until you need them again the next year.

Why Scrapbooking?

A scrapbook is a creative project that appeals to students' artistic sides. It is a fantastic motivational tool. Even reluctant writers will be excited by the prospect of an ongoing arts and crafts project that chronicles their school year.

A scrapbook is not just a memory book. It can also be an excellent tool for enhancing writing skills. Instead of highlighting a variety of photos and items, the pages of this scrapbook will highlight writing. In essence, students will use written descriptions to mentally create the pictures that are not being used.

Students at any grade level can make a scrapbook, and it can be linked to all subjects in the curriculum. Scrapbook pages can be created using journaling, lists, labels, letters, paragraphs, or the more formal narrative, persuasive, and expository writing. Writing is not just for language arts; assignments can be written for math, social studies, and science to display in the scrapbook. Small projects and student work that have been exhibited in the hallway or on a bulletin board can also be artistically displayed on scrapbook pages.

Motivating Students

Ideally, all of your students will be excited when you announce a new writing assignment. However, this doesn't seem to be the case for all students, especially reluctant writers. *Scrapbooking Student Writing* can be the motivator that you are looking for! Use the prospect of an arts and crafts project to motivate students to complete their writing assignments. Before assembling each page in this book, students must first complete a writing assignment. Entice them to do their best work on their writing by showing them the sample of the assembled page that they will have created once they finish the assignment. Knowing that a piece of writing will be incorporated into their scrapbooks can help to inspire students. Hopefully, during future lessons in writing instruction, you will hear, "Will this be a page in our scrapbooks?" or, "Let's put this in our scrapbooks!"

Finding the Time

Helping students improve their writing skills is an important part of any curriculum. Scrapbooking is simply a motivator to practice these critical skills. Like many other skills, students improve their writing through practice. The more reasons you can find for students to write, the better. That's why this book includes writing assignments for every area of the curriculum. And, most of the pages in this book can be used for a variety of writing assignments, not just the two options that are provided. If you have an assignment in mind, select a page layout and have students follow the assembly instructions.

Planning and organization are the keys to saving time for any lesson presented in the classroom. A few minutes of teacher preparation will save valuable class time. Gather and organize supplies before students arrive for the day. You can also save time by allocating a specific amount of time each day for the scrapbooking process. Students do not need to complete their entire scrapbook page projects in one day. In fact, it's better that they don't. The writing process alone—prewriting, drafting, revising, editing, and publishing—should take a few class sessions. The bulk of the time should be devoted to writing since that is the true focus of the scrapbooking project.

There are 36 scrapbook page projects in this book, one for each week of the school year. You can devote a small portion of time each day or a longer period of time for two to three days. It all depends on what is best for your classroom schedule. Students can also complete portions of the projects at home. For example, they might complete prewriting and begin drafting one day and then finish their first drafts for homework that night. You can assign coloring as homework and complete the assembly process together as a reward for a job well done.

Supply List

The basic supplies for creating a student scrapbook are already found in most classrooms, and many of them can be shared among students. Gather the following supplies before beginning the first scrapbook project.

✳ **Paper**
Students will use paper for the background of each scrapbook page and to add frames and mats to decorate their pages. You can choose to use 8½" x 11" (21.5 cm x 28 cm) card stock, colorful copy paper, or construction paper. Scrapbookers usually use card stock because it is sturdy; it will not fade; and it is acid free, so it will not damage photographs over time. It can also be used in a copy machine. Card stock is the most expensive of the three options, but it can be purchased in bulk, and it is useful for a variety of craft projects throughout the school year. Copy paper can also be used in a copy machine, but it is not as sturdy as card stock. Construction paper is the most budget-friendly option, but it cannot be used in a copy machine, and it fades over time. Construction paper is larger than standard paper, so it will have to be cut to fit in a binder.

✳ **1½" (3.75 cm) binder with a clear plastic front pocket for each student**
You can purchase these in bulk or ask parents to provide the binders by including it on your classroom supply list.

✳ **3-hole punch**

✳ **Camera** (and film if not using a digital camera)

✳ **Scissors**

✳ **Markers (fine tip and broad tip) and/or colorful pencils**

✳ **Pencils**

✳ **Pens** (optional for writing assignments)
You may want students to complete writing assignments using pencils, in which case pens will not be necessary.

✳ **Glue or glue sticks**

✳ **Rulers**

✳ **Large envelopes or resealable plastic bags**
Students will use these to store pieces of incomplete scrapbook projects.

Optional Extra Supplies

This list provides suggestions for extra items to embellish scrapbook pages. While none of them are required, you might want to add pizzazz to a few special pages throughout the year. (For examples, see some of the sample pages throughout this book.) You can find most of these supplies at craft stores and specialty scrapbooking stores. You can also find several of these items at office supply stores. Or, consider sending a note home to families—they might be able to donate or loan some of their own supplies to the class.

* **8½" x 11" (21.5 cm x 28 cm) clear plastic page protectors**
  One page protector can display two scrapbook pages if the layouts are placed back-to-back. They will protect the pages, and the scrapbooks will last longer.

* **Paper cutter**

* **Patterned paper**
  Patterned paper is available in 8½" x 11" (21.5 cm x 28 cm) and 12" x 12" (30.5 cm x 30.5 cm). It costs more than standard paper, but several students can share one piece. Use the paper sparingly for accents, title matting, or cutting out letters. Patterned paper can be purchased in single sheets or in discounted bulk packs. (Or, students can create their own patterned paper by following the directions on page 15.)

* **Decorative-edge scissors**
  Decorative-edge scissors are available in a variety of patterns, but "deckle edge" scissors are the easiest for students to use because they do not have a repeating pattern that needs to be lined up when making multiple cuts.

* **Decorative punches** (hole punchers that cut small shapes and designs)

* **Clip art** (CDs, preloaded on your computer, or found online)

* **Die-cuts**
* **Stickers**

* **Gift tags**
* **Buttons**

* **Rubber stamps and ink pads**
* **Fabric scraps**

* **Yarn**
* **Raffia**

* **Ribbon**
* **Gel pens**

* **Decorated stationery or small notepads**
* **Pigment ink markers** (These do not fade over time.)

* **Glitter**
* **Snap-on grommets**

Scrapbooking on a Budget

Anyone can scrapbook—even on a budget! Scrapbooking can be an expensive endeavor, especially if you purchase all of the special papers, tools, and embellishments that are available. However, your students can create masterpieces on a budget using basic classroom supplies and a few occasional embellishments. Following are some tips for keeping the cost to a minimum.

* **Use construction paper for backgrounds.**
  Construction paper can ruin a copy machine, so it won't be useful for reproducing the clip art in this book. However, you can use construction paper for the background of each scrapbook page instead of the more costly card stock. It isn't as sturdy as card stock and it will fade over time, but it certainly serves as an excellent substitute when budget is an issue. If you are using binders, it will also need to be cut to fit because standard construction paper is larger than a binder.

* **Use a 3-hole punch instead of page protectors.**
  If you are using binders, use the 3-hole punch and place the scrapbook pages directly into the binders instead of using clear plastic page protectors. The protectors will help preserve the scrapbook longer, but this is one place you can save a few dollars.

* **Make construction paper covers instead of using binders.**
  Instead of spending your budget on binders, use construction paper and laminate the front and back covers. Use the 3-hole punch and attach the pages together using paper fasteners, ribbon, or yarn. This makes it easy to add pages as the year progresses. And, you won't need to cut the construction paper to fit in the binders, so you will save time, as well.

* **Ask families for donations.**
  Send home a letter asking families to check their craft supplies and scraps for any items that could be donated to the class. Paper scraps, buttons, and pieces of ribbon are great accents for a scrapbook page!

* **Ask local wallpaper stores for sample donations.**
  Many wallpaper stores have books of discontinued paper samples that make excellent scrapbook embellishments. Often, they will donate old books if you ask.

* **Purchase "extras" that can be used more than once.**
  Instead of spending most of your budget on expendable supplies, consider purchasing tools that can be used repeatedly, such as decorative-edge scissors, punches, and rubber stamps. You will get more out of your investment and can reuse the supplies year after year.

Getting Started

First, review this book and familiarize yourself with the topics of the scrapbook pages. *Scrapbooking Student Writing* includes instructions, writing assignments, and clip art to make 36 scrapbook pages, one for each week of the school year. Pages do not have to be completed in any particular order—use the pages in the order that works best for your class.

When you have selected a page, peruse the sample assembled page to familiarize yourself with the project. Review the materials list, assembly directions, and teacher tips. Then, select a writing assignment and make a copy of the necessary clip art page(s) on white copy paper for each student. Gather the necessary supplies. If you are providing any extra supplies (see Optional Extra Supplies, page 9), gather those, as well.

Display the sample assembled page for students as you explain the project. Remind them that they will first complete the writing assignment. Then, they will decorate and assemble their own scrapbook pages.

Explain the writing assignment and help students begin the brainstorming process. Have each student complete the steps of the writing process— prewriting, drafting, revising, and editing—before she publishes the assignment by copying it in her best handwriting onto her scrapbook template. It is a good idea for students to copy their completed writing onto the scrapbook templates using pencils in case they make mistakes. Then, they can trace the writing with a pen or fine-tipped marker. (Or, they can leave the writing in pencil. It is not necessary to trace the writing.)

When the writing is complete, provide students with all of the supplies they need to color and cut out the clip art. Then, have them assemble their scrapbook pages using the directions provided. Remind students that they do not need to copy the sample assembled page. Each student should color the clip art and decorate his page any way he chooses. Each scrapbook should be a unique expression of the student who makes it!

Once the pages are complete and the glue is dry, help students put them into their scrapbook binders. Store the scrapbooks in the classroom until the end of the year. They make excellent end-of-the-year gifts for families!

Tips & Suggestions

Following are some general tips and suggestions for staying organized, saving time, and scrapbooking like a seasoned professional.

Organization

* Use a page protector or resealable plastic bag to store pieces of an incomplete page inside a student's binder.

* Keep a file folder for each page that is created. Store the corresponding pages from this book in the files. Or, put all of the pages in a binder. Also, include any sample assembled pages that you create as alternative samples to display for students.

* Keep any leftover materials in the file with the corresponding pages from this book. The leftover materials should be given to students who were absent on the day that the class began a new scrapbook page.

* Keep scraps of card stock, construction paper, and patterned paper organized in resealable plastic bags or clear, plastic storage boxes. Often, only a small piece of paper is needed, and these scraps are a perfect fit. For efficient organization, separate the scraps by color and/or size.

Time Management

* Unless the writing activity is short, students probably won't be able to complete the writing process and the scrapbook page layout on the same day. Usually the writing needs revision, so it's best to plan to tackle the page layout a few days after students begin the writing process.

* To save time in the classroom, have students complete their final writing drafts and/or some of the coloring as homework. Then, help students assemble their finished scrapbook pages the next day in class.

* Organize all of the supplies for a project before students arrive for the day. Arrange the supplies in a way that works best for your classroom setup. For example, the supplies can be placed on a tray for each student group; separated into resealable plastic bags, file folders, or large envelopes to distribute to each student; or arranged on a long table for students to walk along "buffet style" and pick up what they need.

* Have students make the scrapbook covers (pages 38–40) after school pictures are taken. Then, each student can use a wallet-sized photo for the cover picture.

Titles and Words

* Instead of using the titles from the clip art pages in this book, titles can be generated on the computer using a variety of fonts and colors. Students can print the titles on colorful copy paper or card stock. Or, the titles can be printed in black ink on white copy paper and then copied onto colorful card stock. If the font is an outline font, students can color the title.

* If a student is writing a title, label, or other piece of writing for a page, have him first print lightly with a pencil. This prevents wasted paper because any mistakes can be easily erased. Once the spelling and arrangement of the lettering are correct, have the student retrace the letters with a fine-tip marker or pen.

* For creative titles, give students small die-cut shapes, such as squares, circles, or stars, and have them write a letter on each shape. Other small shapes, such as apples, pumpkins, or leaves, can also be used.

* Let students write the first letter of a title, or the first letter of each word of a title, on small die-cut shapes.

* Draw or trace small shapes or letter outlines on white copy paper. Then, use a copy machine to copy the design onto patterned paper or card stock. Let students cut out the shapes or letters to use for titles and labels.

* Do not put construction paper through a copier or printer. Construction paper can ruin a copy machine or printer because of the small particles it may leave behind.

* Instead of using the titles provided on the clip art pages, let students write their own creative titles using lettering techniques (pages 16–17). Have students practice using the techniques on scrap paper before they use them on actual scrapbook layouts. The more comfortable they are with the techniques, the fewer mistakes they will make on good paper. Also, remind them to draw everything lightly with a pencil before tracing the letters with colorful markers.

* If students are writing titles or labels using lettering techniques (pages 16–17), tell them it is OK for letters to be crooked. It is difficult to draw letters in a straight line, especially for children! And, randomly tilting the letters makes them look like they are more playful and have personality.

Miscellaneous

✳ Encourage students to look at a sample assembled page only to get ideas about the theme. Students should choose their own colors and layout designs to make the pages unique. At first, they might want to copy the samples until they become more comfortable with scrapbooking. But, remind them that they can design their layouts any way that they want!

✳ Most of the pages described in this book do not use photographs, but for those that do, use an acid free background paper so that the photos will not be damaged over time.

✳ Have students use markers or colorful pencils when coloring their layouts. Crayons include chemicals that can damage a layout over time.

✳ Remind students to be careful when coloring large areas with markers. Wet marker can transfer to hands and then smudge the layout.

✳ If a student is working on a piece of writing and she finds that she doesn't have enough room on the writing template, encourage her to keep writing! Provide lined paper and let her finish her writing. Then, mat the piece of lined paper on colorful paper and adhere it to a second piece of background paper to create a two-page scrapbook layout. Or, if you don't want to use a second piece of background paper, glue the matted lined paper to the back of the scrapbook page.

✳ Students can practice their computer skills by typing the final drafts of their writing, either at home or at school. Encourage them to use fun fonts and ink colors! Then, each student can cut around the writing and glue it onto a writing template.

✳ As much as possible, have students write on copy paper or scraps of card stock instead of writing on the background paper. This will keep them from wasting entire sheets of paper if they make mistakes. Also, writing directly on heavyweight papers can make indentations that do not erase.

✳ If a student is writing directly on a scrapbook page and he makes a mistake with a marker or pen, have him rewrite the words on a separate scrap of colorful paper or card stock. Then, tell him to glue that scrap on top of the mistake. It will look like it was meant to be there!

✳ Distribute copies of pages 15–17 for students to use as a reference when decorating their scrapbook pages.

Decorative Techniques

For an easy and cost-effective way to add pizzazz to any scrapbook page, have students draw simple decorative designs in the empty spaces of the background area. They can also add interest by drawing borders (also called *penstitching*) around photos, titles, and templates. Encourage them to use a variety of colors to draw some of the following designs or to create their own. Or, enlarge one of the Make-Your-Own Background Paper patterns found throughout this book and provide copies for students. Have students trace and color the light gray patterns with colorful markers to create their own background papers. Consider printing the patterns on colorful copy paper, as well.

three-dot pattern   swirl pattern   asterisk pattern

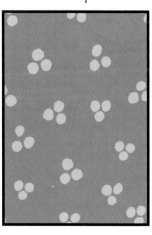 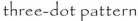 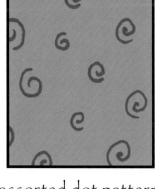

star pattern   assorted dot pattern   mixed pattern

 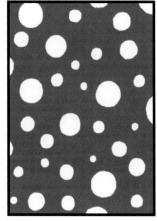 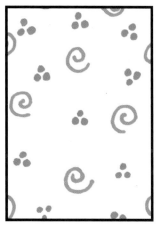

Penstitching Techniques

1. ▬ ▬ ▬ ▬ ▬ ▬ ▬   3. ●●●●●●●●● ●

2. ▬ ▭▭▭▭▭▭   4. ● ▬ ● ▬ ● ▬ ●

Lettering Techniques

There are many simple types of lettering that can easily be used to add a unique, personal touch to a scrapbook page. Following are a few easy-to-use lettering techniques.

Use die-cuts or small shapes.

Add dots or other shapes to the ends and corners of letters.
(If you wish, draw the dots or shapes in a different color than the letters.)

Add lines to the ends and corners of letters.

Add swirls to the ends and corners of letters.

   Scrapbooking Student Writing ✽ CD-104163

Draw an open space on one side of each letter.
(Fill the space with a pattern or a solid color.)

Add outline penstitching to any letter, word, or title.

Draw bubble letters with round or smooth edges.

Step 1: Lightly write the letters with a pencil. Leave space between the letters.

Step 2: Outline each letter.

Step 3: Erase the letters inside the outlines. Fill each letter with a pattern.

Directions for Assembly:

1. Instruct students to color the clip art. If they prefer, they can write their titles on white paper instead of using the clip art titles.

2. Have students cut out all of the art.

3. Tell them to carefully glue their titles and "best thing" frames onto the mat paper (optional). They may need to cut the mat paper to fit the art.

4. Ask students to arrange the pieces on their background paper before they start gluing. When everything is ready, let them carefully glue the pieces in place.

Teacher Tips:

1. Use these instructions when completing all of the monthly wrap-up pages (pages 19–37). Separate instruction pages are not provided for each month.

2. Keep a list in your plan book of memorable events that occur during the month. Then, you can help students during the brainstorming process.

3. Remind students to be descriptive and use expressive vocabulary.

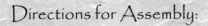

Monthly Wrap-Ups

Each Student Needs:

- 1 piece of background paper
- 1 copy of corresponding clip art page
- ½ page of paper to mat the title and "best thing" frame (optional)
- pencil
- markers or colorful pencils
- scissors
- glue or glue stick
- any additional embellishments you wish to provide

Writing Assignment:

Have each student brainstorm a list of 8–10 memorable things that happened during the month. Tell students to include things that happened both at school and at home.

Option 1: Have students neatly copy their lists onto their large writing templates. Then, in the "best thing" frame, have each student write a few sentences or a short paragraph about her favorite thing on her list.

Option 2: Have each student write his favorite event from the brainstorming list in his "best thing" frame. Tell each student to write a paragraph in the large writing template that describes his favorite event. Or, he can write about the event as a journal entry, describing it as if he is reliving the moment.

Super September

The best thing about September was . . .

getting my new dog, Dusty! He
is still a puppy, but he weighs
over 50 pounds! We like to play
catch with him and take him to
the park.

We went on a field trip to the zoo.
My team won a game of capture the flag in P.E.
I met my new friend, Jenny.
We got a new dog named Dusty.
I finished reading a good book.
My brother turned four.
I started taking karate.
My sister was in a dance recital.
We learned about our solar system.
I lost a tooth.

Super September

The best thing about September was . . .

© Carson-Dellosa • CD-104163 • Scrapbooking Student Writing

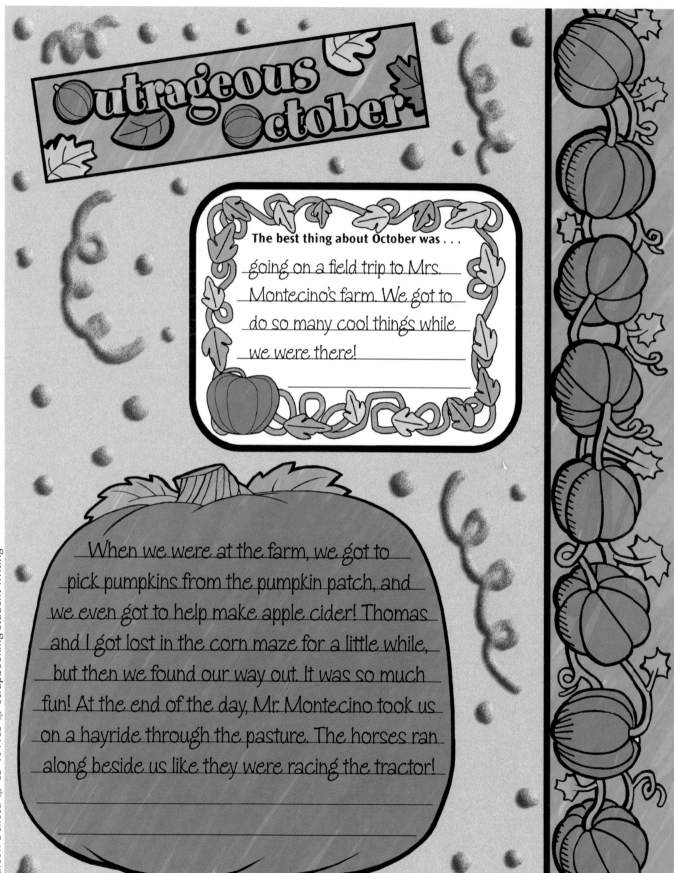

Outrageous October

The best thing about October was . . .

going on a field trip to Mrs. Montecino's farm. We got to do so many cool things while we were there!

When we were at the farm, we got to pick pumpkins from the pumpkin patch, and we even got to help make apple cider! Thomas and I got lost in the corn maze for a little while, but then we found our way out. It was so much fun! At the end of the day, Mr. Montecino took us on a hayride through the pasture. The horses ran along beside us like they were racing the tractor!

Outrageous October

The best thing about October was . . .

© Carson-Dellosa ✳ CD-104163 ✳ Scrapbooking Student Writing

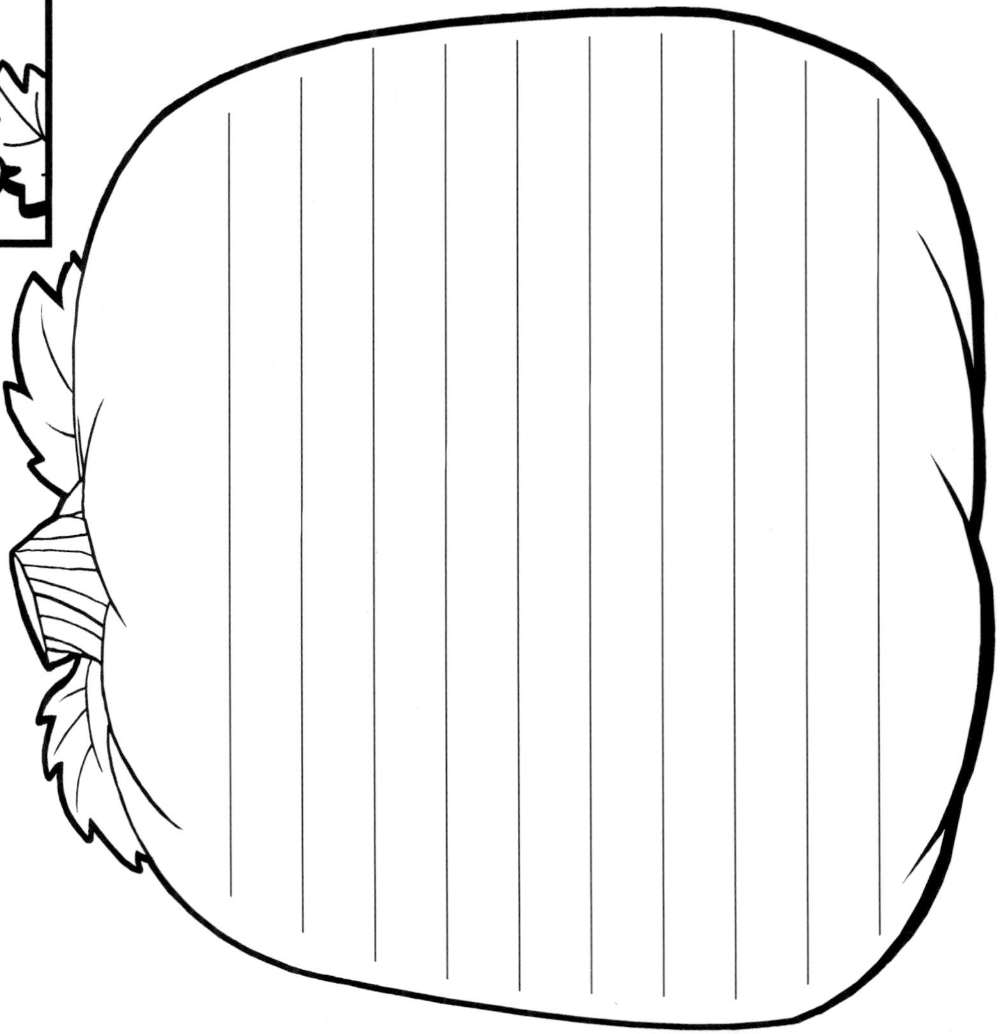

Newsworthy November

My sister was born.

I moved into a new bedroom.

Nana and Papa came for Thanksgiving.

We ate a yummy Thanksgiving dinner.

I was in our town's Thanksgiving Day parade.

I was named Artist of the Week at school.

Our teacher e-mailed us pictures of her vacation.

It snowed 13 inches in one day!

We made snowmen on the playground.

We ate pumpkin pie at school.

The best thing about November was . . .

when Nana and Papa came.
They helped with baby Maria,
and I got to play with my mom.
Grandma cooked a lot, and I
helped her bake a pie.

Newsworthy November

The best thing about November was . . .

24

The best thing about December was . . .

visiting my family in Minnesota

during the holidays. I love the snowy

weather there!

_____

_____

It took us eight hours to drive to Minnesota to visit my grandparents, aunts, uncles, and cousins. But, it was worth it! Every year during our visit, my cousins and I put on a play for the family. This year, I was the director! Our family always loves our play. Sometimes we create plays about things we learned in school. Other times, we make up our plays by ourselves. I like it better when we make up our own plays. It is so much fun!

Dazzling December

The best thing about December was . . .

26

Jazzy January

The best thing about January was . . .

when the power went out.
Mom let us roast marshmallows
and hot dogs in the fireplace. She
read a book to us by candlelight.
We watched Dad chop wood.

The power went out during a storm.
My teacher, Mr. Stefano, got married.
They painted a mural in the hall of our school.
Seth brought his groundhog for show-and-tell.
My parents had a New Year's Eve party.
I broke my finger playing basketball.
We sold doughnuts to raise money at school.
The Panthers won the Super Bowl.
My class went ice skating.
I lost two teeth.

Jazzy January

The best thing about January was . . .

© Carson-Dellosa ✳ CD-104163 ✳ Scrapbooking Student Writing

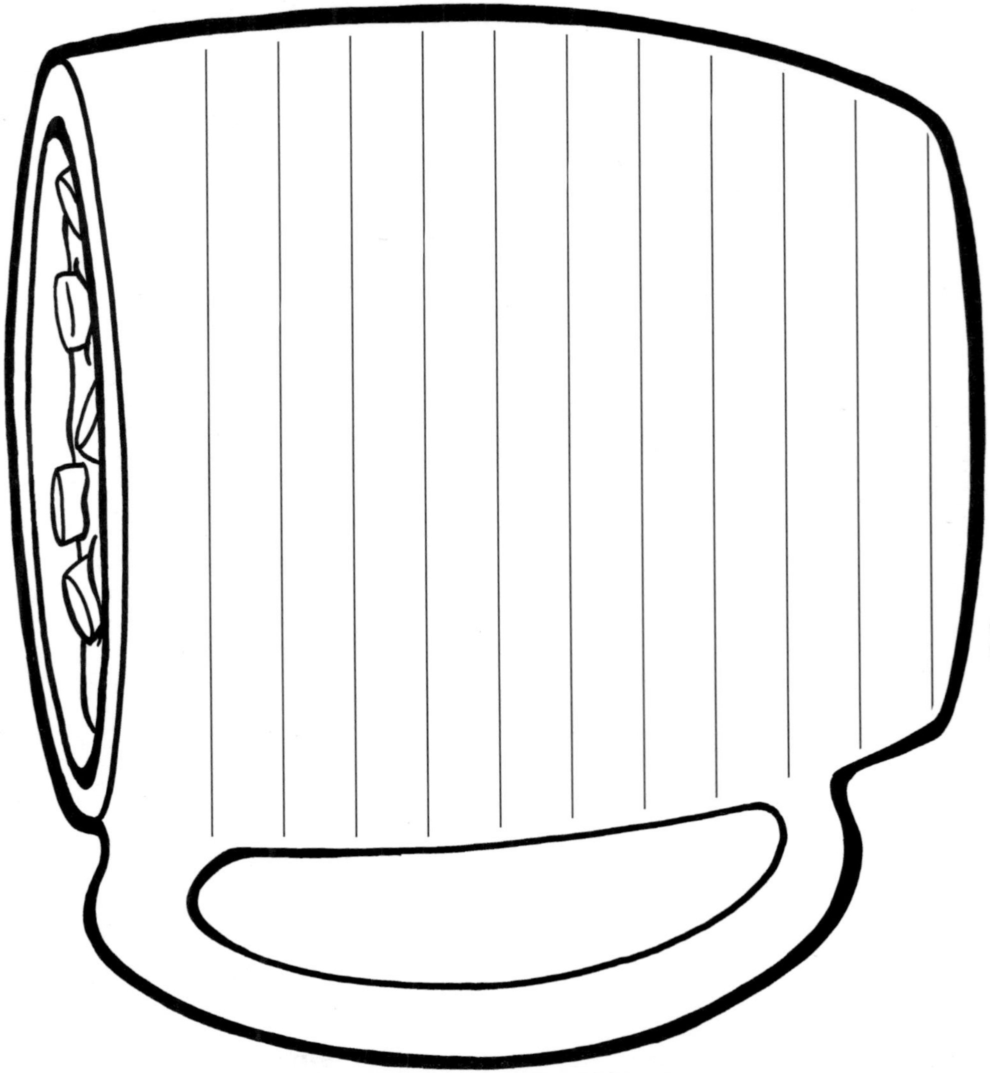

Fantastic February

I got a lot of valentine candy!

My valentines were all homemade.

I got an A in math on my report card.

My brothers had their pictures in the newspaper.

We painted my room yellow and red.

My friend Shane moved down the street from us.

I got chicken pox.

I started a social studies project about my state.

We went skiing in the mountains.

I joined a basketball team at the youth center.

The best thing about February was . . .

going skiing. I finally got to ride the ski lift and go down the slope by myself while my dad watched. I fell a lot, but it was still fun!

Fantastic February

The best thing about February was . . .

30

The best thing about March was . . .

I turned 10 years old! My parents planned a surprise party for me at my favorite restaurant. Then, they took us to see a cool movie.

Magnificent MARCH

I had my tenth birthday!

We learned how to play racket ball in P.E.

I forgot to wear green on St. Patrick's Day!

We flew kites one day during recess.

I got a 95 on a hard reading test.

My family went camping during spring break.

I got a letter from my sixth-grade pen pal.

My teacher found a lost kitten.

We saw a big rainbow in the sky.

Magnificent MARCH

The best thing about March was . . .

© Carson-Dellosa ✳ CD-104163 ✳ Scrapbooking Student Writing

Amazing APRIL

The best thing about April was . . .

getting to go on my first trip in an airplane! It was so exciting to fly up in the air and see everything down below us.

I went to a birthday party at the skating rink.

I won second place in my gymnastics meet.

My brother turned 16.

I helped my mom bake a cake for my brother.

Nana and Papa came to visit.

I flew on an airplane for the first time.

We learned about types of governments.

We studied rocks and minerals.

My friends and I had a sleepover.

Amazing
APRIL

The best thing about April was . . .

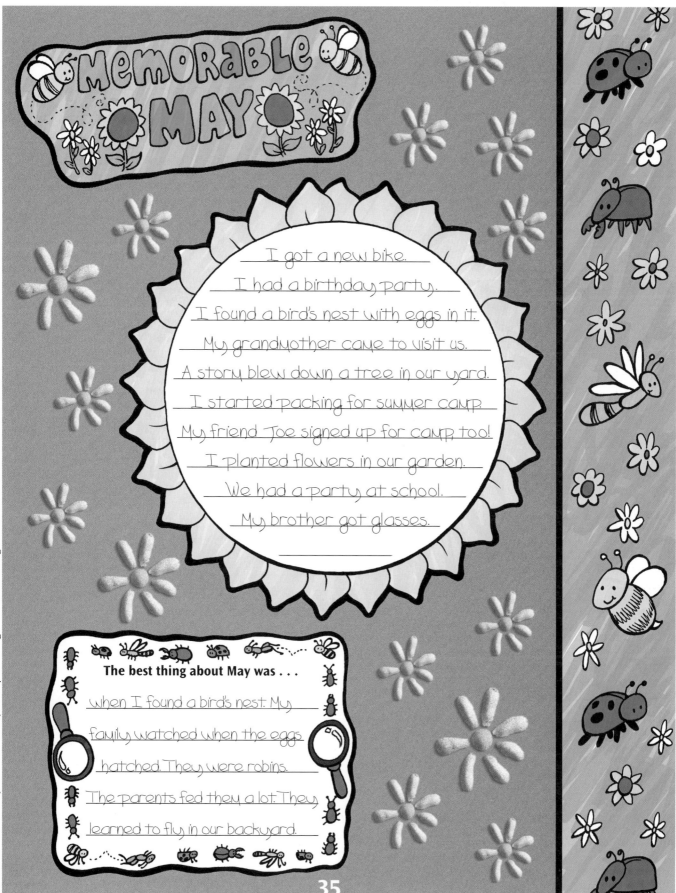

Memorable MAY

I got a new bike.

I had a birthday party.

I found a bird's nest with eggs in it.

My grandmother came to visit us.

A story blew down a tree in our yard.

I started packing for summer camp.

My friend Joe signed up for camp, too!

I planted flowers in our garden.

We had a party at school.

My brother got glasses.

_____

The best thing about May was . . .

when I found a bird's nest. My
family watched when the eggs
hatched. They were robins.
The parents fed them a lot. They
learned to fly in our backyard.

MeMORaBLe MaY

The best thing about May was . . .

36

My Third-Grade Scrapbook

by Sarah Green
2006–2007

38

Scrapbook Cover

Each Student Needs:

- 1 piece of background paper
- 1 copy of clip art (page 40)
- 1 student photo
- ¼ page of paper to mat the photo
- pencil
- markers or colorful pencils
- scissors
- glue or glue stick
- any additional embellishments you wish to provide

Teacher Tips:

1. Consider waiting until students have become comfortable with the scrapbooking process before having them assemble their covers. Their covers will look much better!

2. When a student writes directly on his page, have him first print lightly with a pencil and then carefully trace over it with a marker.

3. If a student makes a mistake writing in marker, have her rewrite the words on a separate scrap of colorful paper and glue it over the mistake. It will look like it was meant to be there!

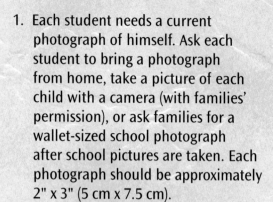

Directions for Assembly:

1. Each student needs a current photograph of himself. Ask each student to bring a photograph from home, take a picture of each child with a camera (with families' permission), or ask families for a wallet-sized school photograph after school pictures are taken. Each photograph should be approximately 2" x 3" (5 cm x 7.5 cm).

2. Instruct students to color the clip art (page 40). If they prefer, they can write their titles on scrap paper instead of using the clip art titles.

3. Have students cut out all of the art.

4. Tell them to carefully glue their photographs onto the mat paper. They may need to cut the mat paper to fit the photographs.

5. Ask students to arrange the pieces on their background paper before they start gluing. When everything is ready, let them carefully glue the pieces in place.

6. Finally, have each student write her byline and the school year on her cover with a pencil (for example, *by Sarah Green, 2006–2007*). Have students trace over the pencil lines with markers.

7. Have each student place her cover in the plastic pocket on the front of her binder.

8. If you are not using binders, laminate the covers to protect the inside pages and make the books look more professional. You will also need to laminate paper to use for back covers.

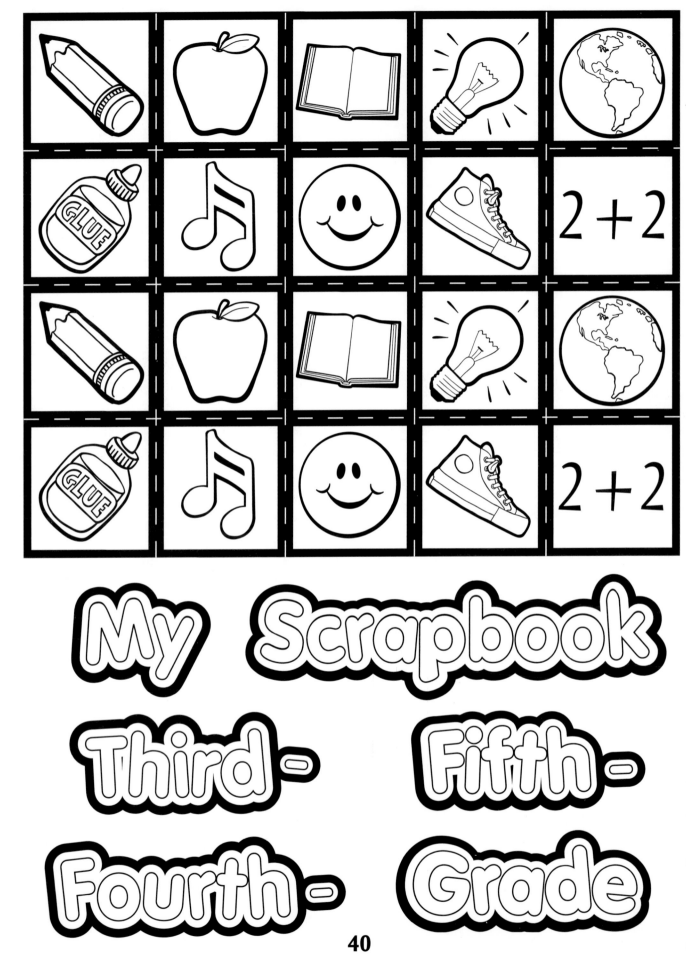

My Scrapbook

Third-
Fourth-

Fifth-
Grade

First Day

First Day
of School
September 5, 2006

GLUE

of School

© Carson-Dellosa ✻ CD-104163 ✻ Scrapbooking Student Writing

Third Grade

Hello!
My name is
Hannah

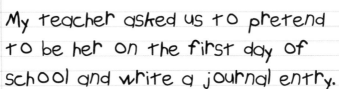

My teacher asked us to pretend
to be her on the first day of
school and write a journal entry.

Today is the first day of school.
I am so excited to be a teacher!
I spent weeks decorating the
classroom and getting materials
ready. I cannot wait to meet my
students! I hope they like me. I know
we are going to have a fun year.
I bet they are really smart.

Directions for Photo Shoot:

1. Place a student desk and chair in front of a wall or bulletin board that you have decorated for the first day of school. The bulletin board will serve as a backdrop for the photo shoot.

2. Place a "First Day of School" sign on top of the desk or attach it to the front.

3. Decorate the desk with classroom items, such as a cup of pencils, a stapler, and an apple.

4. Take a picture of each student sitting at the desk.

5. If you use a digital camera, print each picture using a color printer. Each picture should be approximately 4" x 4" (10 cm x 10 cm).

6. If you use an instant camera, keep the pictures in a safe place while they develop.

7. Distribute the pictures to students after they have completed the writing assignment and when it is time to assemble the scrapbook pages.

First Day of School

The Teacher Needs:

- camera
- film (if not using a digital camera)
- computer and color printer (if using a digital camera)
- student desk and chair
- teacher-made "First Day of School" sign
- classroom items to decorate the desk
- bulletin board decorated for the first day of school

Teacher Tips:

1. Students probably won't have time to complete the entire scrapbooking process on the first day of school. Have students start working on the writing assignment while you are taking the pictures. When you finish the pictures, give them time to complete their writing or ask them to finish it at home.

2. Complete the assembly process on the second day of school or sometime that week.

3. Consider laminating the "First Day of School" sign to save and reuse next year.

© Carson-Dellosa ✳ CD-104163 ✳ Scrapbooking Student Writing

First Day of School

1. Instruct students to color the clip art (page 46). If they prefer, they can write their titles on white paper instead of using the clip art titles.

2. Have students cut out all of the art.

3. Tell them to carefully glue their photos and journal entries onto the mat paper. They can also mat the titles. They may need to cut the mat paper to fit their photos and text.

4. Ask students to arrange the pieces on their background paper before they start gluing. When everything is ready, let them carefully glue the pieces in place.

5. Finally, have students write the date of the first day of school below their photographs.

Teacher Tip:

If you are not using the name tags that students wore on the first day of school, have each student use the name tag clip art provided on page 46.

Each Student Needs:

- 2 pieces of background paper
- 1 copy of clip art (page 46)
- 1 student photo
- 1 piece of paper to mat photo and text
- lined paper
- pencil
- markers or colorful pencils
- scissors
- glue or glue stick
- first day of school name tag (optional)
- any additional embellishments you wish to provide

Writing Assignment:

Prompt students by asking them how they felt when they woke up on the first day of school. Encourage students to think of descriptive words for their feelings. Then, ask them if they think teachers have those feelings, too!

Option 1: On lined paper, have each student write a journal entry about how she felt on the first day of school. Tell her to include what she thinks about the upcoming year. Encourage advanced writers to include breakfast-table dialogue with correct punctuation.

Option 2: On lined paper, have each student write a journal entry as if he were a teacher on the first day of school. Remind him to include descriptions of his thoughts, worries, and hopes for the school year.

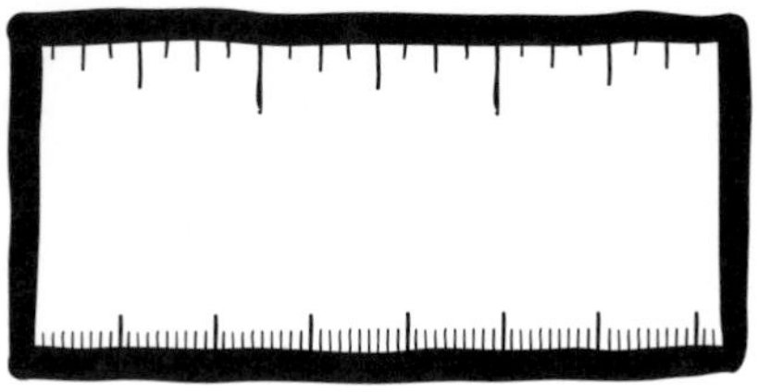

Hello!
My name is

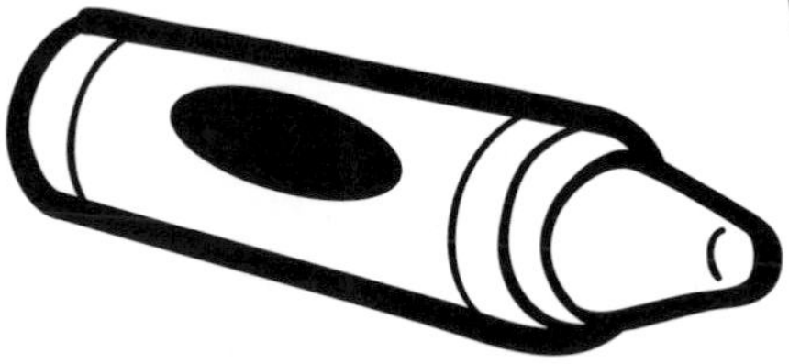

First Day of School

GLUE

Third

Fourth

Fifth

Grade

46

Happy Birthday to Me!

The best birthday party theme would be . . .
a movie star party where we get to dress up in fancy clothes and pretend to be stars! I would definitely dress as my favorite actress.

The best birthday cake would be . . .
a triple chocolate ice cream cake. I love chocolate, and ice cream is the best!

The best birthday surprise would be . . .
for my best friend Sophie to get to come to my party. She moved to Utah last summer, and I really miss her.

The best birthday gift would be . . .
a computer. We get to use the computers at school, and I really love learning to type. I hope I get one to use for homework and e-mails!

Directions for Assembly:

1. Instruct students to color the clip art (page 49 or 50). If they prefer, they can write their titles on white paper instead of using the clip art titles.

2. Have students cut out all of the art.

3. Tell them to carefully glue their titles onto the mat paper (optional). They may need to cut the mat paper to fit their titles.

4. Ask students to arrange the pieces on their background paper before they start gluing. When everything is ready, let them carefully glue the pieces in place.

Teacher Tips:

1. Consider providing students with small pieces of wrapping paper or ribbon scraps to use for page embellishments.

2. Suggest that students use colorful pencils to lightly shade the writing area on the gift boxes instead of coloring them with markers so that their writing will be visible. Or, have them leave the writing area white and only color around the perimeter of the words.

3. If you choose Writing Option 2 and students need additional room, provide lined paper and let them attach it to the backs of their scrapbook pages. Or, students can each use an additional piece of background paper and create a second page for their scrapbooks. Each student can mat the writing on a different color piece of paper to add interest.

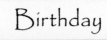

Birthday

Each Student Needs:

- 1 piece of background paper
- 1 copy of clip art (page 49 or 50, not both)
- ¼ page of paper to mat title (optional)
- pencil
- markers or colorful pencils
- scissors
- glue or glue stick
- any additional embellishments you wish to provide

Writing Assignment:

Option 1: Distribute copies of page 49. Have students fill in the blanks on the four gift boxes to write about their birthdays. Have students include why they chose each of their answers.

Option 2: Distribute copies of page 50. Prompt students to write a story about the birthday party of their dreams. Tell them to include who would be there, what they would do, where they would go, and what kinds of gifts they would receive. Remind them that this doesn't have to be realistic—they can be as creative as they wish! Have each student write his story neatly on the large gift box writing template.

Happy Birthday to Me!

The best birthday gift would be . . .

_____
_____
_____
_____

The best birthday party theme would be . . .

_____
_____
_____
_____
_____

The best birthday surprise would be . . .

_____
_____
_____

The best birthday cake would be . . .

_____
_____
_____

49

Happy Birthday to Me!

Personality Wheel

Harriet likes to write and think a lot. She reads all of the time.

She says funny things about people even when they are mean to her.

She likes to hide and watch people when they don't know she is there.

She is always spying and writing.

Harriet never sees her parents and her friends get mad at her.

Harriet only gets caught spying one time.

smart

funny

sneaky

busy

lonely

quiet

Harriet M. Welch
from
Harriet the Spy

Directions for Assembly:

1. Instruct students to color the clip art (page 54).

2. Have students cut out the art.

3. Ask students to arrange their Personality Wheels on their background paper before they start gluing. When everything is ready, let them carefully glue their Personality Wheels in place.

Teacher Tips:

1. Consider printing the copies of page 54 on colorful paper so that students will not need to color the large wheel using markers or colorful pencils.

2. If you choose Writing Option 2 and students need additional room, provide lined paper and let them attach it to the backs of their scrapbook pages. Or, students can each use an additional piece of background paper and create a second page for their scrapbooks. Each student can mat the writing on a different color piece of paper to add interest.

Personality Wheel (Option A)

Each Student Needs:

- 1 piece of background paper
- 1 copy of clip art (page 54)
- lined paper (if using Writing Option 2)
- pencil
- markers or colorful pencils
- scissors
- glue or glue stick
- any additional embellishments you wish to provide

Writing Assignment:

Option 1: Have students fill in their Personality Wheels. First, each student should write her name in the center circle. Then, in the small spaces, she should write six traits that are part of her personality, such as *neat*, *silly*, *organized*, *loud*, *kind*, and *artistic*. Finally, in the remaining areas of the wheel, she should write examples of how she exhibits each trait. For example, if the trait is *loud*, she might write, *I like to sing so loudly that it makes my dog howl.*

Option 2: Have students fill in their Personality Wheels as described above. Then, ask them to write stories on lined paper that describe one or more of their personality traits in detail. Have more advanced writers focus on paragraph structure, grammar, punctuation, and proper use of dialogue.

© Carson-Dellosa ✳ CD-104163 ✳ Scrapbooking Student Writing

Personality Wheel (Option B)

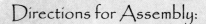

Each Student Needs:

- 1 piece of background paper
- 1 copy of clip art (page 54)
- lined paper (if using Writing Option 2)
- pencil
- markers or colorful pencils
- scissors
- glue or glue stick
- any additional embellishments you wish to provide

Directions for Assembly:

1. Instruct students to color the clip art (page 54).

2. Have students cut out the art.

3. Ask students to arrange their Personality Wheels on their background paper before they start gluing. When everything is ready, let them carefully glue their Personality Wheels in place.

Teacher Tip:

If students need additional room, provide lined paper and let them attach it to the backs of their scrapbook pages. Or, students can each use an additional piece of background paper and create a second page for their scrapbooks. Each student can mat the writing on a different color piece of paper to add interest.

Writing Assignment:

Option 1: Instruct students to fill in their Personality Wheels about their favorite literary characters. First, each student should write the chosen character's name in the center. Then, in the small spaces, he should write six traits that are part of the character's personality, such as *funny*, *weird*, *bossy*, *annoying*, *forgetful*, and *disorganized*. Finally, in the remaining areas, he should write examples of how the character exhibits each trait. For example, if the trait is *bossy*, a student might write, *Mary Jane is bossy because she always tells her brother what to do, like the time she made him play dolls with her even though he wanted to play outside.*

Option 2: Have students fill in their Personality Wheels for literary characters as described above. Then, ask them to pretend they are the characters they selected. On lined paper, have each student write a journal entry from the character's perspective and include information that shows at least two of the personality traits described on the wheel.

My School

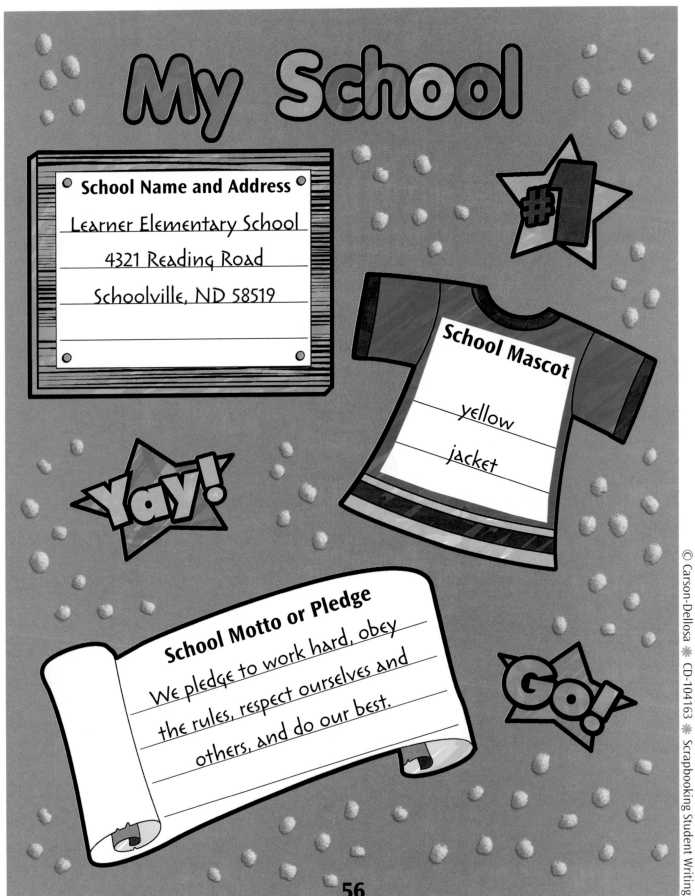

School Name and Address

Learner Elementary School

4321 Reading Road

Schoolville, ND 58519

#1

School Mascot

yellow

jacket

Yay!

School Motto or Pledge

We pledge to work hard, obey the rules, respect ourselves and others, and do our best.

Go!

56

Is Great!

We have music class and art class every week.

#1

We get to read good books in class.

My teacher is smart and funny.

Go!

Yay!

My friends and I get to play together at recess.

Directions for Assembly:

1. Instruct students to color the clip art (pages 59–60). If they prefer, they can write their titles on white paper instead of using the clip art titles.

2. Have students cut out all of the art.

3. Tell them to carefully glue their titles onto the mat paper (optional). They may need to cut the mat paper to fit their titles.

4. Ask students to arrange the pieces on their background paper before they start gluing. When everything is ready, let them carefully glue the pieces in place.

Teacher Tip:

If you choose Writing Option 2, consider having students mat their writing on different color pieces of paper to add interest.

My School Is Great!

Each Student Needs:

- 2 pieces of background paper
- 1 copy of clip art (page 59)
- 1 copy of clip art (page 60)
- ½ page of paper to mat title (optional)
- lined paper (if using Writing Option 2)
- pencil
- markers or colorful pencils
- scissors
- glue or glue stick
- any additional embellishments you wish to provide

Writing Assignment:

Option 1: Instruct students to fill in the templates on page 59. You may need to provide copies of the school song or motto/pledge, especially for younger students. Have students write a few sentences in each megaphone that describe why they think their school is great.

Option 2: Instruct students to fill in the templates on page 59 as described above. Then, have each student write a letter on lined paper to a potential new student describing why his school is so fantastic and fun. Remind students to be descriptive and try to include anecdotal stories that convey why they enjoy their school. Have students write brief sentences or paragraphs in the megaphones that highlight aspects of their school.

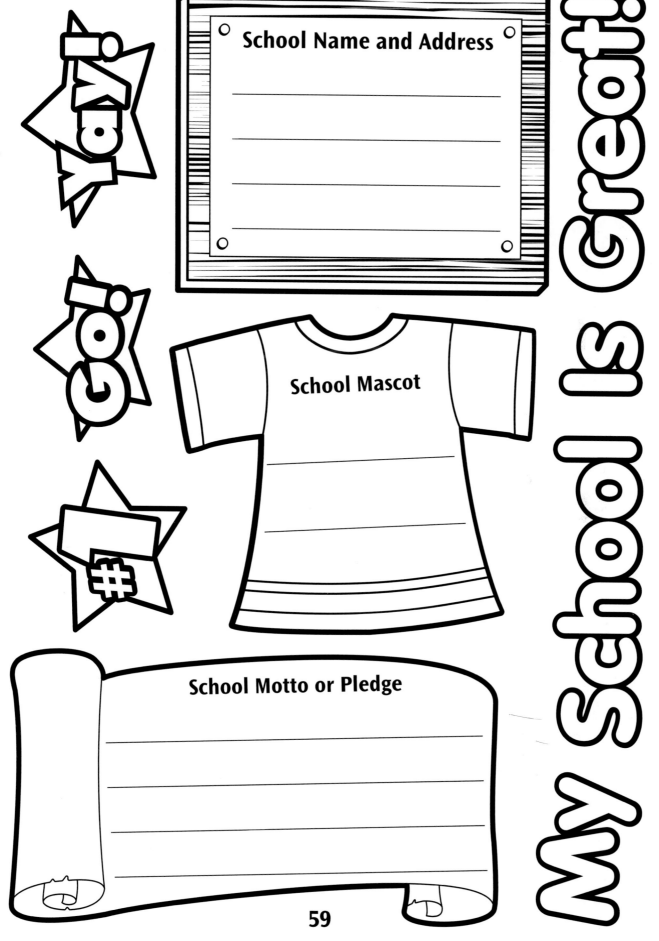

Yay!

School Name and Address

_____

_____

_____

_____

Go!

School Mascot

#

School Motto or Pledge

_____

_____

_____

_____

My School Is Great!

59

© Carson-Dellosa ✹ CD-104163 ✹ Scrapbooking Student Writing

© Carson-Dellosa ✳ CD-104163 ✳ Scrapbooking Student Writing

A Helping Hand

Each Student Needs:

- 1 piece of background paper
- 1 copy of clip art (page 64)
- ½ page of paper to mat title (optional)
- lined paper (if using Writing Option 2)
- pencil
- markers or colorful pencils
- scissors
- glue or glue stick
- any additional embellishments you wish to provide

Writing Assignment:

Option 1: Encourage students to brainstorm lists of ways they help others. Lists can include things done at school or outside of school. Tell each student to choose her top five helpful activities and write them on the fingers of the large handprint.

Option 2: Have students fill in their large handprints as described above. Then, ask them to write stories on lined paper that describe one or more of the things they listed on the large handprints. Remind them that they should be proud of their top five helpful activities, and they should be descriptive in their explanations of why they are proud of themselves!

Directions for Assembly:

1. Instruct students to color the clip art (page 64). If they prefer, they can write their titles on white paper instead of using the clip art titles.

2. Have students cut out all of the art.

3. Tell them to carefully glue their titles onto the mat paper (optional). They may need to cut the mat paper to fit their titles.

4. Ask students to arrange the pieces on their background paper before they start gluing. When everything is ready, let them carefully glue the pieces in place.

Teacher Tips:

1. Consider printing the copies of page 64 on various shades of paper so that students will not need to color the large handprint using markers or colorful pencils.

2. Instead of using the large handprints that are provided, students can trace their own hands onto colorful paper. If you choose this option, make sure that their handprints are large enough to write on each finger.

3. If you choose Writing Option 2 and students need additional room, provide lined paper and let them attach it to the backs of their scrapbook pages. Or, students can each use an additional piece of background paper and create a second page for their scrapbooks. Each student can mat the writing on a different color piece of paper to add interest.

A Helping Hand

I am helpful when...

My favorite game is . . .
chess. I really want
to beat my dad
someday!

My favorite season is . . .
summer because I love
to go to the beach
and play in
the water.

My favorite food is . . .
pizza, especially when
the cheese is hot
and gooey!

My favorite place is . . .
the beach. My brother
and I like to build
sand castles.

66

My favorite book is
Because of Winn-Dixie
by Kate DiCamillo. It
is about a girl and
her dog.

My favorite animal is . . .
a dog. I especially
love my dog, Rufus.
He is funny!

My favorite dessert is
a banana split made
with ice cream, hot
fudge, and cherries!

My favorite color is
green because it
reminds me of summer.

My favorite sport
is baseball. I play
shortstop on my team.

My favorite song is . . .
"Surfin' U.S.A." by The
Beach Boys because I'm
going to learn to surf
next summer!

Directions for Assembly:

1. Instruct students to color the clip art (pages 69–70). If they prefer, they can write their titles on white paper instead of using the clip art titles.

2. Have students cut out all of the art.

3. Tell them to carefully glue their titles onto the mat paper (optional). They may need to cut the mat paper to fit their titles.

4. Ask students to arrange the pieces on their background paper before they start gluing. When everything is ready, let them carefully glue the pieces in place.

Teacher Tips:

1. Consider printing the copies of pages 69–70 on colorful paper so that students will not need to color the smiley faces using markers or colorful pencils.

2. Brainstorm a list of prompts for the blank smiley faces so that you will be ready if students have trouble thinking of topics.

3. If you choose Writing Option 2, consider having students mat their writing on different color pieces of paper to add interest.

4. If you choose Writing Option 2 and students need additional room, provide lined paper and let them attach it to the backs of their scrapbook pages. Or, students can each use an additional piece of background paper and create another page for their scrapbooks. Each student can mat the writing on a different color piece of paper to add interest.

What Makes Me Smile?

Each Student Needs:

- 2 pieces of background paper
- 1 copy of clip art (page 69)
- 1 copy of clip art (page 70)
- ½ page of paper to mat title (optional)
- lined paper (if using Writing Option 2)
- pencil
- markers or colorful pencils
- scissors
- glue or glue stick
- any additional embellishments you wish to provide

Writing Assignment:

Option 1: Instruct students to fill in the smiley faces on pages 69–70 by completing the sentences about some of their favorite things. Tell them to fill in the blank smiley faces with sentences about other favorite things that are not already listed. Remind them to use complete sentences. Also, if there is room on the smiley faces, have each student write a second sentence that tells why he selected the "favorite."

Option 2: Instruct students to fill in the smiley faces as described above. Then, tell them to choose two or three of the most interesting topics. Have them write paragraphs on lined paper that describe these favorite things or funny stories about how these things became their favorites.

68

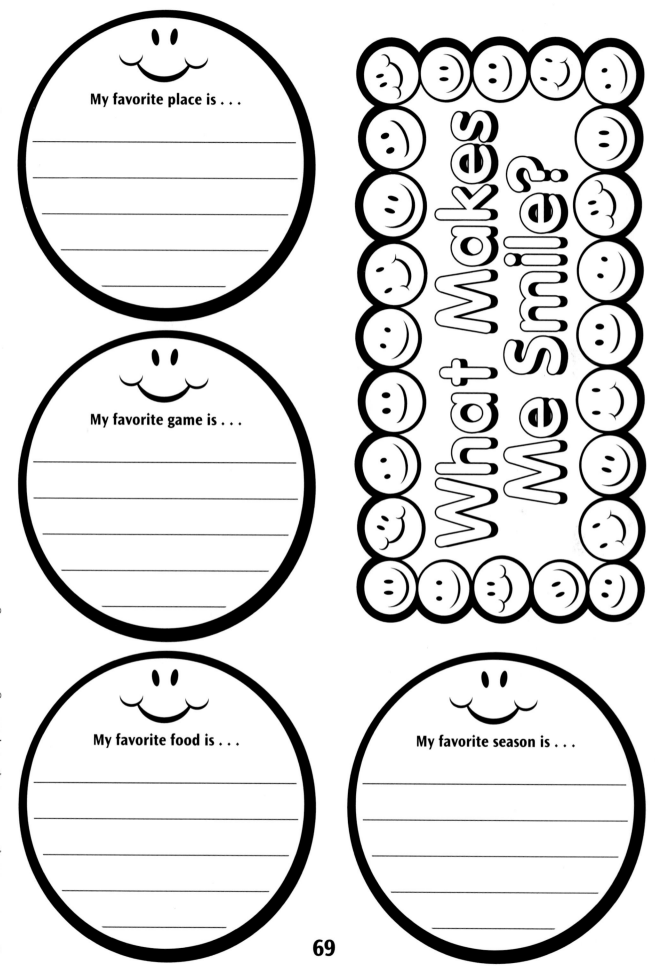

My favorite place is . . .

My favorite game is . . .

What Makes Me Smile?

My favorite food is . . .

My favorite season is . . .

My favorite animal is . . .

My favorite song is . . .

One of my "battiest" traits is that I love to sing karaoke. My parents got a machine last year, and I love it! My favorite thing to do is dress up and sing Elvis Presley songs!

Another "batty" thing about me is that I don't like sweets. Have you ever met a kid who didn't like candy?! Well, you have now. My mom says I'm destined to have good teeth because of my weird trait.

I think the "battiest" thing about me is that I can pick up things with my toes. I'm even trying to teach myself to hold a pencil and write my name with my toes! Isn't that crazy?

As for things that "drive me batty," I think the biggest one is when my four-year-old sister colors in my notebooks. It makes me so crazy!!!

The other thing that drives me "batty" is when I can't find my baseball glove. I know it's my fault for never putting it away where it belongs, but it still drives me crazy when I need it and I can't find it.

Directions for Assembly:

1. Instruct students to color the clip art (page 73 or 74). If they prefer, they can write their titles on white paper instead of using the clip art titles.

2. Have students cut out all of the art.

3. Tell them to carefully glue their titles onto the mat paper (optional). They may need to cut the mat paper to fit their titles.

4. Ask students to arrange the pieces on their background paper before they start gluing. When everything is ready, let them carefully glue the pieces in place.

Teacher Tips:

1. Suggest that students use colorful pencils to lightly shade the writing area on the bats instead of coloring them with markers so that their writing will be visible. Or, have them leave the writing area white and only color around the perimeter of the words.

2. Remind students that bats can be shades of brown, too, not just black!

3. If you choose Writing Option 2, consider having students mat their writing on different color pieces of paper to add interest.

"Batty" Facts About Me

Each Student Needs:

- 1 piece of background paper
- 1 copy of clip art (page 73 or 74, not both)
- ½ page of paper to mat title (optional)
- lined paper (if using Writing Option 2)
- pencil
- markers or colorful pencils
- scissors
- glue or glue stick
- any additional embellishments you wish to provide

Writing Assignment:

Discuss the meaning of the word "batty" (crazy or silly). Ask students what it means when someone says, "That drives me batty!" Use this discussion as a starter for one of the writing options below.

Option 1: Distribute copies of page 73. Have students fill in the bats with "batty" facts about themselves. Or, they might choose to write sentences about things that "drive them batty." Remind them to use complete sentences.

Option 2: Distribute copies of page 74. Prompt students to write short stories or journal entries on lined paper that describe two or three of their "battiest" traits. Remind them to be descriptive and use good supporting details. Or, let them write about a time when something really "drove them batty."

74

Shopping List:

turkey
stuffing
salad
potatoes
green beans
macaroni and cheese
rolls
pumpkin pie
apple pie

Recipe for a Great Thanksgiving

Mashed Potatoes:
Peel a bag of potatoes. Boil them. Put them in a pot without any water in it. Mash them up with lots of butter and milk. Put them in a bowl so that they look nice.

Rolls:
Take the plastic bag out of the freezer. When they are soft, put the rolls on a pan in the sun to rise. When they get big, bake the rolls in the oven for 10 minutes.

76

© Carson-Dellosa ✿ CD-104163 ✿ Scrapbooking Student Writing

One of my favorite family traditions is when we go around the table and we all say what we are thankful for.

My aunts, uncles, and cousins always come for Thanksgiving, and we play a game of football. It is really fun to work up a big appetite before we sit down to eat!

After dessert, my cousins and I usually play games while our parents watch a movie. It's really exciting when I win, but even when I don't, it's still fun to play.

Directions for Assembly:

1. Instruct students to color the clip art (pages 79–80). If they prefer, they can write their titles on white paper instead of using the clip art titles.

2. Have students cut out all of the art.

3. Tell them to carefully glue their titles onto the mat paper (optional). They may need to cut the mat paper to fit their titles.

4. Ask students to arrange the pieces on their background paper before they start gluing. When everything is ready, let them carefully glue the pieces in place.

Teacher Tips:

1. This assignment should be completed at school. If students take it home, they might get help from family members, and the recipes won't be nearly as unique!

2. Provide a list of transition words, such as first, second, third, next, then, finally, etc., for students to use when writing the steps of their recipes.

3. If you choose Writing Option 2, consider having students mat their writing on different color pieces of paper to add interest.

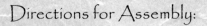

Thanksgiving

Each Student Needs:

- 2 pieces of background paper
- 1 copy of clip art (page 79)
- 1 copy of clip art (page 80, if using Writing Option 1)
- ½ page of paper to mat title (optional)
- lined paper (if using Writing Option 2)
- pencil
- markers or colorful pencils
- scissors
- glue or glue stick
- any additional embellishments you wish to provide

Writing Assignment:

Lead students in a brainstorming session about what makes a great Thanksgiving. All responses do not have to be about the meal—students can talk about family, friends, traditions, sports, etc., as well.

Option 1: Have each student fill in the recipe cards and shopping list (page 79) with her version of how to prepare a great Thanksgiving feast. Then, have her fill in the recipe cards (page 80) with things that are part of a great Thanksgiving. These should be "recipes" for activities, not foods.

Option 2: Have students fill in page 79 as directed above. Then, have each student write a story on lined paper about the best Thanksgiving he ever had. Or, he might choose to write a story about his ideal Thanksgiving.

Shopping List:

Recipe for a Great Thanksgiving

Where in the World Are We?

My school's address is . . .

MOUNTAIN CITY
ELEMENTARY SCHOOL
4206 APRIL LANE

SCHOOL

Map

My school is in the city (or town) of . . .

MOUNTAIN
CITY

X

My country is on the continent of . . .

NORTH
AMERICA

My state (or province) is in the country of . . .

THE UNITED
STATES
OF AMERICA

My city (or town) is in the state (or province) of . . .

WYOMING

Directions for Assembly:

1. Instruct students to color the clip art (page 83 or 84). If they prefer, they can write their titles on white paper instead of using the clip art titles.

2. Have students cut out all of the art.

3. Tell them to carefully glue their titles onto the mat paper (optional). They may need to cut the mat paper to fit their titles.

4. Ask students to arrange the pieces on their background paper before they start gluing. When everything is ready, let them carefully glue the pieces in place.

Teacher Tips:

1. Suggest that students use colorful pencils to lightly shade the writing areas instead of coloring them with markers. Or, have them leave the writing area white and only color around the perimeter of the words.

2. For a challenge, have students find a picture of their state or province's flag. Tell them to draw and color the flag on a piece of paper. If you choose this option, have students mat their flags and display them as described in Teacher Tip 3.

3. If you choose Writing Option 2 and students need additional room, provide lined paper and let them attach it to the backs of their scrapbook pages. Or, students can each use an additional piece of background paper and create a second page for their scrapbooks. Each student can mat the writing on a different color piece of paper to add interest.

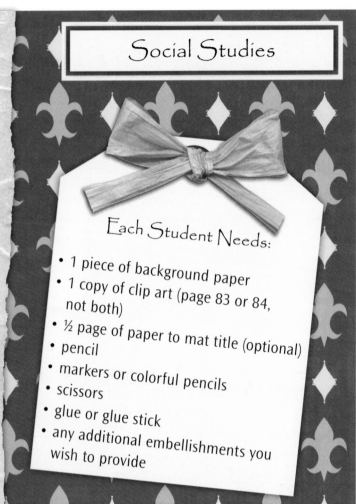

Social Studies

Each Student Needs:

- 1 piece of background paper
- 1 copy of clip art (page 83 or 84, not both)
- ½ page of paper to mat title (optional)
- pencil
- markers or colorful pencils
- scissors
- glue or glue stick
- any additional embellishments you wish to provide

Writing Assignment:

Option 1: Distribute copies of page 83. Instruct students to fill in the blanks on each piece of clip art to tell where their school is located in the world. They may need to do some research to fill in all of the blanks.

Option 2: Distribute copies of page 84. Instruct each student to use the "Did You Know . . ." template to write a flyer detailing why tourists should visit his city or town. Tell them to include fun facts, sights to see, restaurants to try, etc.

Where in the World Are We?

Map

My school is in
the city (or town) of . . .

My state (or province)
is in the country of . . .

SCHOOL

My school's address is . . .

My city (or town)
is in the state (or province) of . . .

My country
is on the continent of . . .

Did You Know . . .

Where in the World Are We?

84

① art
② social studies
③ reading
④ science

This week's number one hit goes back to the beginning of time. It has been a favorite of cave dwellers, Renaissance people, and many creative individuals of the modern era. I love art because it lets me express myself and share with others. So, enjoy this week's number one hit: art!

Directions for Assembly:

1. Instruct students to color the clip art (page 87 or 88). If they prefer, they can write their titles on white paper instead of using the clip art titles.

2. Have students cut out all of the art.

3. Tell them to carefully glue their titles onto the mat paper (optional). They may need to cut the mat paper to fit their titles.

4. Ask students to arrange the pieces on their background paper before they start gluing. When everything is ready, let them carefully glue the pieces in place.

Teacher Tips:

1. The Top of the Charts page is intended to be used for writing about favorite school subjects, but it can be used to rank anything—favorite sports, television shows, extracurricular activities, music, foods, etc. Or, it could even be used for least favorites or pet peeves.

2. Some of the most creative writing begins with a topic that inspires the author. When the author feels strongly about a topic, she will most likely use more descriptive and animated vocabulary.

Top of the Charts

Each Student Needs:

- 1 piece of background paper
- 1 copy of clip art (page 87 or 88, not both)
- ½ page of paper to mat title (optional)
- pencil
- markers or colorful pencils
- scissors
- glue or glue stick
- any additional embellishments you wish to provide

Writing Assignment:

Option 1: Distribute copies of page 87. On the small jukeboxes, have each student write one of his four favorite school subjects, with jukebox number one as his favorite. In the remaining lines on each jukebox, have students write a few sentences about why they like each subject.

Option 2: Distribute copies of page 88. Have each student write her four favorite school subjects in order, with number one as her favorite. In the remaining space on the jukebox, have each student write a story about the number one hit subject as if she is a radio announcer presenting this week's number one song. Explain to students that an announcer would tell why the hit is so popular, who likes the hit, how it became so popular, and any other interesting facts about it. (Refer to the sample paragraph on page 85 if students need an example.)

© Carson-Dellosa ✳ CD-104163 ✳ Scrapbooking Student Writing

Top of the Charts

1:

the Charts

2:

3:

4:

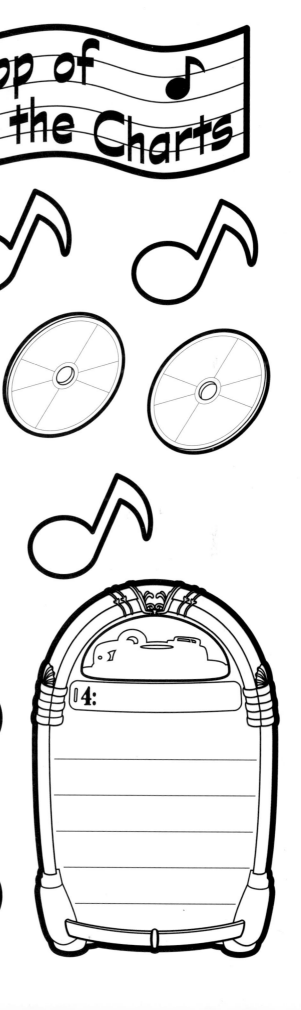

© Carson-Dellosa ✳ CD-104163 ✳ Scrapbooking Student Writing

I'm proud of myself because . . .

I help my mom take care of my baby brother every day after school.

Proud as a Peacock!

I helped my brother learn to ride his bike.

I won the boys' 100 meter dash at field day.

I worked all day helping my uncle fix the fence and earned $10.00!

I painted a picture, and my mom had it framed to hang on the wall!

I learned to do the backstroke.

I passed my water safety certification test.

I earned my first-aid badge at camp.

I started taking golf lessons, and my coach said I was a natural!

Directions for Assembly:

1. Instruct students to color the clip art (pages 91–92). If they prefer, they can write their titles on white paper instead of using the clip art titles.

2. Have students cut out all of the art.

3. Tell them to carefully glue their titles onto the mat paper (optional). They may need to cut the mat paper to fit their titles.

4. Ask students to arrange the pieces on their background paper before they start gluing. When everything is ready, let them carefully glue the pieces in place.

Teacher Tips:

1. Suggest that students use colorful pencils to lightly shade the writing area on the pieces of art instead of coloring them with markers so that the writing will be visible. Or, have them leave the writing area white and only color around the perimeter of the words.

2. If they wish, students can create two fanned layers of feathers. Tell them to glue only the tips of the top layer of feathers so that they can be lifted to read the bottom layer.

3. If you choose Writing Option 2 and students need additional room, provide lined paper and let them attach it to the backs of their scrapbook pages. Or, students can each use an additional piece of background paper and create a second page for their scrapbooks. Each student can mat the writing on a different color piece of paper to add interest.

4. Students can use this page to highlight any achievements that make them proud—not just successes at school!

Proud as a Peacock!

Each Student Needs:

- 1 piece of background paper
- 1 copy of clip art (page 91)
- 1 copy of clip art (page 92)
- ½ page of paper to mat title (optional)
- lined paper (if using Writing Option 2)
- pencil
- markers or colorful pencils
- scissors
- glue or glue stick
- any additional embellishments you wish to provide

Writing Assignment:

Option 1: Tell students to think of things that make them proud. Tell them to focus on things other than grades and classroom successes. They might be proud of themselves for learning to juggle, jumping off the high diving board, or learning to play chess. Tell them to write about their successes in complete sentences on the peacock feathers. They will write about one success on each feather. Have each student write something that she is especially proud of in the "I'm proud of myself because . . ." feature box.

Option 2: Have students fill in the feathers and the feature box as described above. Then, ask them to write explanations on lined paper that describe one or more of the things they listed on the peacock feathers.

Proud as a Peacock!

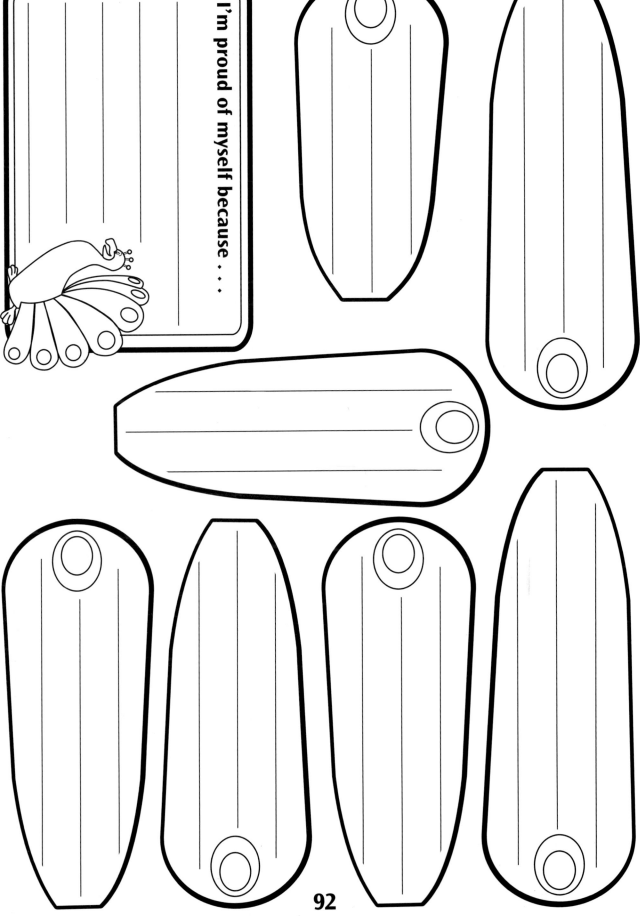

I'm proud of myself because . . .

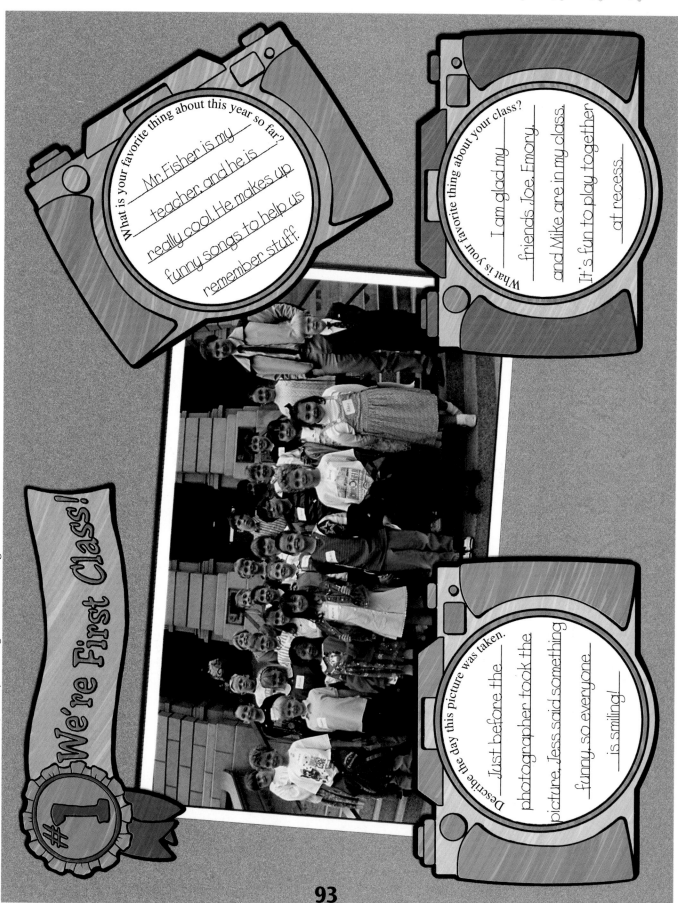

What is your favorite thing about this year so far?

Mr. Fisher is my teacher, and he is really cool. He makes up funny songs to help us remember stuff.

What is your favorite thing about your class?

I am glad my friends Joe, Emory, and Mike are in my class. It's fun to play together at recess.

Describe the day this picture was taken.

Just before the photographer took the picture, Jess said something funny so everyone is smiling!

We're First Class!

#1

Directions for Assembly:

1. Instruct students to color the clip art (page 95 or 96). If they prefer, they can write their titles on white paper instead of using the clip art titles.

2. Have students cut out all of the art.

3. Tell them to carefully glue their titles and photos onto the mat paper (optional). They may need to cut the mat paper to fit their titles and photos.

4. Ask students to arrange the pieces on their background paper before they start gluing. When everything is ready, let them carefully glue the pieces in place.

Teacher Tips:

1. Use a class photo that was taken by you or a volunteer so that you will not infringe on any copyrights. Obtain permission from families to take photos of students.

2. Scan the photo. Use a color printer to make a 4" x 6" (10 cm x 15 cm) copy for each student. Or, use a color photocopier. If these options are not readily available, black and white copies will work, too.

3. If you use black and white copies of the photo, let students color the pictures using colorful pencils. Or, suggest that they color parts of the photos, such as people's clothing.

4. If you choose Writing Option 2 and students need additional room, provide lined paper and let them attach it to the backs of their scrapbook pages. Or, students can each use an additional piece of background paper and create a second page for their scrapbooks. Each student can mat the writing on a different color piece of paper to add interest.

Class Photo

Each Student Needs:

- 1 piece of background paper
- 1 copy of clip art (page 95 or 96, not both)
- 1 copy of a class photo
- 1 piece of paper to mat title and photo (optional)
- pencil
- markers or colorful pencils
- scissors
- glue or glue stick
- any additional embellishments you wish to provide

Writing Assignment:

Option 1: Distribute copies of page 95. Have students fill in the camera templates by writing a few sentences to answer each question.

Option 2: Distribute copies of page 96. Have students fill in the scroll template by writing a story about the day the picture was taken. Maybe a student has a funny story about getting ready for school that day, something silly that happened while getting ready for the photo, or the crazy face that a friend is making in the picture. Or, maybe students will want to write about their class and their favorite things about the year so far.

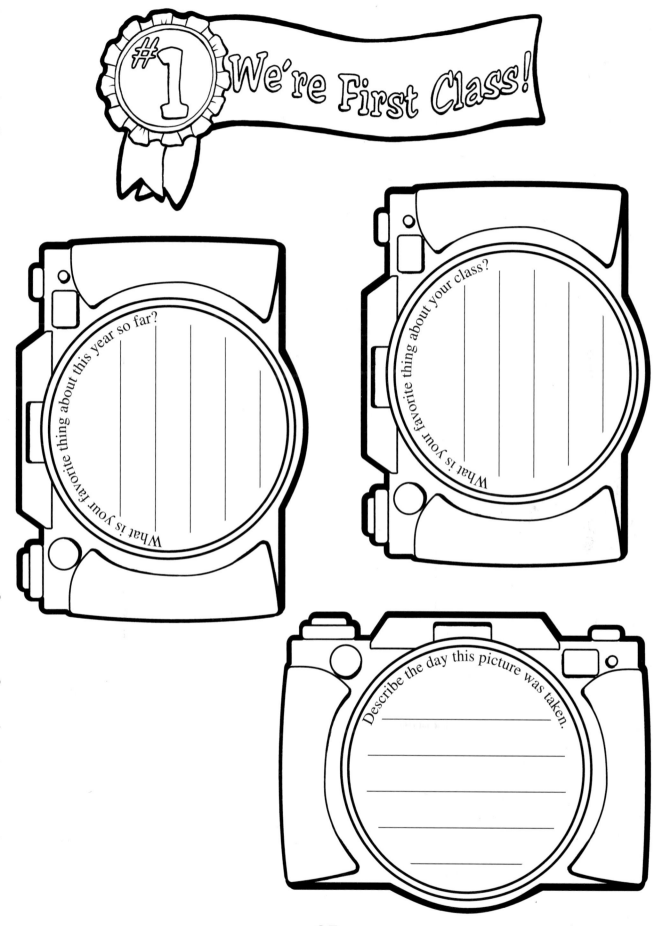

We're First Class!

#1

What is your favorite thing about this year so far?

What is your favorite thing about your class?

Describe the day this picture was taken.

Class Photo

We're First Class!

Directions for Assembly:

1. Instruct students to color the clip art (page 99 or 100). If they prefer, they can write their titles on white paper instead of using the clip art titles.

2. Have students cut out all of the art.

3. Tell them to carefully glue their titles onto the mat paper (optional). They may need to cut the mat paper to fit their titles.

4. Ask students to arrange the pieces on their background paper before they start gluing. When everything is ready, let them carefully glue the pieces in place.

Teacher Tips:

1. Remind students to include the four Ws in their writing—*Who* was involved? *What* happened? *When* did it happen? *Where* did it happen? And, if it is important to add, *How* did it happen?

2. Students can also write about funny things that happened at home, funny family members, or even famous people they think are funny. Or, use this as a chance to review literary characters and ask them to write about particularly funny characters from books or stories they have read.

3. If you choose Writing Option 2 and students need additional room, provide lined paper and let them attach it to the backs of their scrapbook pages. Or, students can each use an additional piece of background paper and create a second page for their scrapbooks. Each student can mat the writing on a different color piece of paper to add interest.

That "Cracks" Me Up!

Each Student Needs:

- 1 piece of background paper
- 1 copy of clip art (page 99 or 100, not both)
- ½ page of paper to mat title (optional)
- pencil
- markers or colorful pencils
- scissors
- glue or glue stick
- any additional embellishments you wish to provide

Writing Assignment:

Discuss the meaning of the phrase, *That cracks me up!*, with students.

Option 1: Distribute copies of page 99. Instruct students to think of funny events that have really "cracked them up" in the classroom or at school. For each funny event, students should write a few sentences in a cracked egg template.

Option 2: Distribute copies of page 100. Instead of writing short sentences in small templates, have each student use the larger template on page 100 to write a story about a funny event or describe a classmate that he thinks is especially funny.

In the year 2007,
I hope to work hard to be
a great student. I would also like
to get my camping badge for scouts.
And, I want to try to learn to ride a
unicycle. But, most of all, I want to go to
the beach for the Fourth of July celebration. They
always have a huge party with great food and fireworks.
It's lots of fun! My friend Cameron and his family
usually get to go with us.

Directions for Assembly:

1. Instruct students to color the clip art (page 103 or 104). If they prefer, they can write their titles on white paper instead of using the clip art titles.

2. Have students cut out all of the art.

3. Tell them to carefully glue their titles onto the mat paper (optional). They may need to cut the mat paper to fit their titles.

4. Ask students to arrange the pieces on their background paper before they start gluing. When everything is ready, let them carefully glue the pieces in place.

Teacher Tips:

1. Consider providing New Year's confetti with the year on it for students to glue to their pages. Or, provide gel pens, glitter pens, or glitter glue to add some sparkle to pages.

2. If you choose Writing Option 2 and students need additional room, provide lined paper and let them attach it to the backs of their scrapbook pages. Or, students can each use an additional piece of background paper and create a second page for their scrapbooks. Each student can mat the writing on a different color piece of paper to add interest.

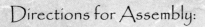

Happy New Year!

Each Student Needs:

- 1 piece of background paper
- 1 copy of clip art (page 103 or 104, not both)
- ½ page of paper to mat title (optional)
- pencil
- markers or colorful pencils
- scissors
- glue or glue stick
- any additional embellishments you wish to provide

Writing Assignment:

Have a discussion with students about New Year's resolutions. Describe what they are and why people make them. Ask students to think of their own New Year's resolutions.

Option 1: Distribute copies of page 103. Have each student write two or three sentences about each of her resolutions on a party hat or balloon template. Also, have her reserve one template to write about why her resolutions are important to her and why she intends to keep them.

Option 2: Distribute copies of page 104. Ask students to think about what they hope to accomplish in the New Year. On the large template, have students write about these aspirations, as well as some of the things that will change for them, such as having another birthday, moving to the next grade in school, growing taller, learning new skills, or going on vacation to new places.

Happy New Year!

W ONDERFUL,
I NTENSE
N EIGHBORHOOD GAMES;
T IMES
E VERYONE
R EMEMBERS.
S NOWY
N IGHTS MAKE
O UR OWN
W INTER WONDERLAND.

Directions for Assembly:

1. Instruct students to color the clip art (page 107 or 108). If they prefer, they can write their titles on white paper instead of using the clip art titles.

2. Have students cut out all of the art.

3. Tell them to carefully glue their titles onto the mat paper (optional). They may need to cut the mat paper to fit their titles.

4. Ask students to arrange the pieces on their background paper before they start gluing. When everything is ready, let them carefully glue the pieces in place.

Teacher Tip:

Provide white or silver sequins, glitter, glitter glue, or gel pens for students to use to embellish their scrapbook pages. A student can also use yarn to accent the mittens or the snowman's scarf or hat.

Winter Break

Each Student Needs:

- 1 piece of background paper
- 1 copy of clip art (page 107 or 108, not both)
- ½ page of paper to mat title (optional)
- pencil
- markers or colorful pencils
- scissors
- glue or glue stick
- any additional embellishments you wish to provide

Writing Assignment:

Option 1: Distribute copies of page 107. Have students think of some of the highlights of winter break. Have each student write two or three sentences about each of his favorite moments or events on a mitten template. Remind students to include funny stories or important moments that made winter break "snow" cool!

Option 2: Distribute copies of page 108. Have students write an acrostic poem using the letters of the word *winter* (or the words *winter snow*). To create an acrostic poem, have each student write the letters of the word *winter* vertically on the left side of the template. Then, instruct her to write a word, phrase, or sentence that starts with each letter of the word *winter*.

Winter Break Was "Snow" Cool!

107

The length
of my hand is . . .
5 1/4 inches. I
think my hand will
be 6 inches long
next year.

My height is . . .
49 inches, or
4 feet 1 inch.
I think I will be
52 inches tall
by next year.

The length
of my hair is . . .
17 inches. I want
to cut my hair so
that it will be
14 inches.

Here's the Scoop!

My shoe size is . . .
13 1/2. I will
probably wear a
size 14 by next
year.

The circumference
of my head is . . .
21 1/2 inches.
I don't think my
head will grow
anymore.

The length
of my foot is . . .
8 inches. My foot
will probably be
1/2 inch longer
next year.

The length of my leg from hip to toe is . . . 27 inches. I think my leg will be 30 inches long by next year.

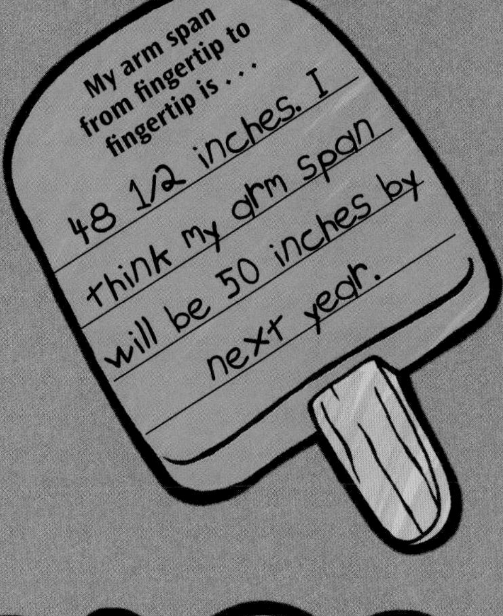

My arm span from fingertip to fingertip is . . . 48 1/2 inches. I think my arm span will be 50 inches by next year.

Some Other Classroom Numbers . . .

1. **Length of the Classroom:** 28 feet

2. **Width of the Classroom:** 16 1/2 feet

3. **Area of the Classroom:** 462 square feet

4. **Number of Windows in the Classroom:** 3

5. **Number of Doors in the Classroom:** 2

6. **Number of Desks in the Classroom:** 27

7. **Number of Chairs in the Classroom:** 32

8. **Number of Bulletin Boards in the Classroom:** 2

9. **Area of the Largest Bulletin Board:** 24 square feet

10. **Number of Steps to the Restroom:** 41

Directions for Assembly:

1. Instruct students to color the clip art (pages 113–114). If they prefer, they can write their titles on white paper instead of using the clip art titles.

2. Have students cut out all of the art.

3. Tell them to carefully glue their titles onto the mat paper (optional). They may need to cut the mat paper to fit their titles.

4. Ask students to arrange the pieces on their background paper before they start gluing. When everything is ready, let them carefully glue the pieces in place.

Teacher Tip:

Have each student use a piece of yarn to measure the circumference of his partner's head. Instruct him to hold the yarn around his partner's head like a headband. Then, he should use a yardstick or meterstick to measure the length of the piece of yarn. This will be the circumference of his partner's head.

Math

Each Student Needs:

- 2 pieces of background paper
- 1 copy of clip art (page 113)
- 1 copy of clip art (page 114)
- ½ page of paper to mat title (optional)
- pencil
- markers or colorful pencils
- scissors
- glue or glue stick
- any additional embellishments you wish to provide

To Be Shared:

- 1 small skein of yarn
- 5–10 yardsticks or metersticks

Writing Assignment:

Option 1: Distribute copies of pages 113–114. Have students work with partners to fill in the blanks. They will need to use yardsticks or metersticks to find most of the measurements. Then, in the space below each sentence, have students predict how much each measurement will change in the next year. For example, a student might write, *The length of my foot is 7 inches.* He might then write, *In one year, I think my foot will be 8.5 inches long.*

Option 2: Distribute copies of pages 113–114. Have students work with partners to fill in the blanks. Then, have them interview classmates to find the largest or smallest measurements. For example, a student might write, *My height is 48 inches.* Then, she might write in the space below the sentence, *Kyle is the tallest person in the class. He is 52 inches tall.*

112

Here's the Scoop!

My height is . . .

The length of my hair is . . . .

The length of my foot is . . .

The length of my hand is . . . .

The circumference of my head is . . .

My shoe size is . . . .

 CD-104163 ✳ Scrapbooking Student Writing

The length of my leg from hip to toe is . . .

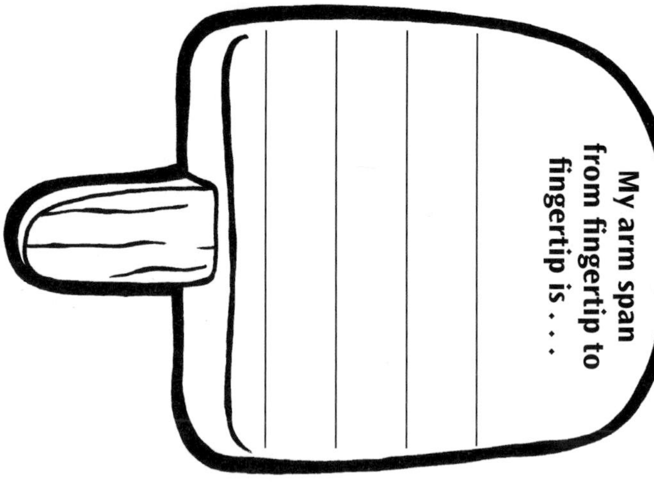

My arm span from fingertip to fingertip is . . .

Some Other Classroom Numbers . . .

1. **Length of the Classroom:** _____

2. **Width of the Classroom:** _____

3. **Area of the Classroom:** _____

4. **Number of Windows in the Classroom:** _____

5. **Number of Doors in the Classroom:** _____

6. **Number of Desks in the Classroom:** _____

7. **Number of Chairs in the Classroom:** _____

8. **Number of Bulletin Boards in the Classroom:** _____

9. **Area of the Largest Bulletin Board:** _____

10. **Number of Steps to the Restroom:** _____

114

F un

R eally cheerful

I nspiring

E ntertaining

N ice

D ependable

S weet

115

Directions for Assembly:

1. Instruct students to color the clip art (page 117 or 118). If they prefer, they can write their titles on white paper instead of using the clip art titles.

2. Have students cut out all of the art.

3. Tell them to carefully glue their titles onto the mat paper (optional). They may need to cut the mat paper to fit their titles.

4. Ask students to arrange the pieces on their background paper before they start gluing. When everything is ready, let them carefully glue the pieces in place.

Teacher Tip:

If you choose Writing Option 2, students can make a list instead of an acrostic poem. Tell students to number the column of hearts. Next to each number, they should write words or short phrases that describe what friendship means to them.

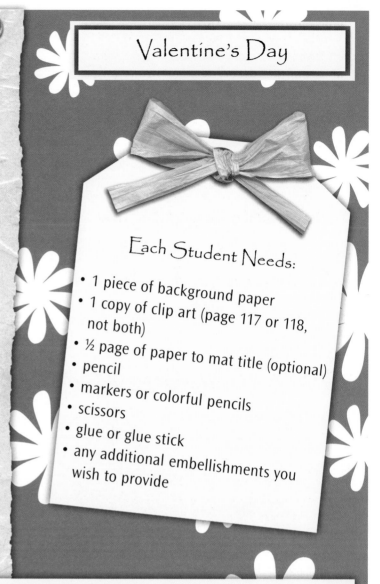

Valentine's Day

Each Student Needs:

- 1 piece of background paper
- 1 copy of clip art (page 117 or 118, not both)
- ½ page of paper to mat title (optional)
- pencil
- markers or colorful pencils
- scissors
- glue or glue stick
- any additional embellishments you wish to provide

Writing Assignment:

Option 1: Distribute copies of page 117. Have students use this page as a place to display special valentines they receive from their classmates. Have each student glue two or three special valentines to her background paper. Then, tell her to write a few sentences on a template about each valentine. She should include who it is from, why it is special, and why she likes it. She should then glue the templates to her paper next to the valentines.

Option 2: Distribute copies of page 118. Have students write an acrostic poem using the letters of the word *friends* or the word *valentine*. First, instruct students to glue the correct number of hearts in a column on the left side of the page. They will need one heart for each letter in the word. To create an acrostic poem, have students write one letter of the word *friends* in each of the hearts. Then, instruct them to write words, phrases, or sentences that start with each letter of the word *friends*.

116

© Carson-Dellosa ✷ CD-104163 ✷ Scrapbooking Student Writing

BEE My Valentine

117

I was respectful when . . .
I held the door for my elderly neighbor. It really helped her because she uses a cane.

I was honest when . . .
I told my aunt when I broke her vase. She was very glad that I told the truth.

Shining STAR!

I was trustworthy when . . .
I took care of my neighbor's dog for a week. He was glad to know Max was in good hands.

I was compassionate when . . .
I brought my cousin soup and movies when she was sick. They helped her feel better.

I was responsible when . . .
I found a wallet at the store and turned it in. The man who lost it was so relieved.

Directions for Assembly:

1. Instruct students to color the clip art (page 121 or 122). If they prefer, they can write their titles on white paper instead of using the clip art titles.

2. Have students cut out all of the art.

3. Tell them to carefully glue their titles onto the mat paper (optional). They may need to cut the mat paper to fit their titles.

4. Ask students to arrange the pieces on their background paper before they start gluing. When everything is ready, let them carefully glue the pieces in place.

Teacher Tips:

1. Discuss the importance of showing good character and talk about the different traits. If necessary, discuss definitions of the character traits that appear on page 121. (*respect:* act of being considerate; *responsibility:* quality of being dependable; *honesty:* quality of being genuine and truthful; *trustworthiness:* quality of deserving trust and confidence; *compassion:* desire to help those who are in need)

2. If students need additional room, provide lined paper and let them attach it to the backs of their scrapbook pages. Or, students can each use an additional piece of background paper and create a second page for their scrapbooks. Each student can mat the writing on a different color piece of paper to add interest.

Good Character

Each Student Needs:

- 1 piece of background paper
- 1 copy of clip art (page 121 or 122, not both)
- ½ page of paper to mat title (optional)
- pencil
- markers or colorful pencils
- scissors
- glue or glue stick
- any additional embellishments you wish to provide

Writing Assignment:

Option 1: Distribute copies of page 121. Have students fill in the star templates by completing each sentence about good character. If space allows, have each student write a second sentence that tells why each act was important.

Option 2: Distribute copies of page 122. Ask each student to think of a time when someone else showed good character toward him. In the star, have him write the character trait or traits that the person exhibited. In the box, have him write about the event, describing what happened and who was involved. Each student should also write about how he felt and how he was affected when the other person showed good character toward him. If space allows, have each student include what he learned about the importance of showing good character.

Shining STAR!

I was respectful when . . .

I was honest when . . .

I was responsible when . . .

I was trustworthy when . . .

I was compassionate when . . .

Shining STAR!

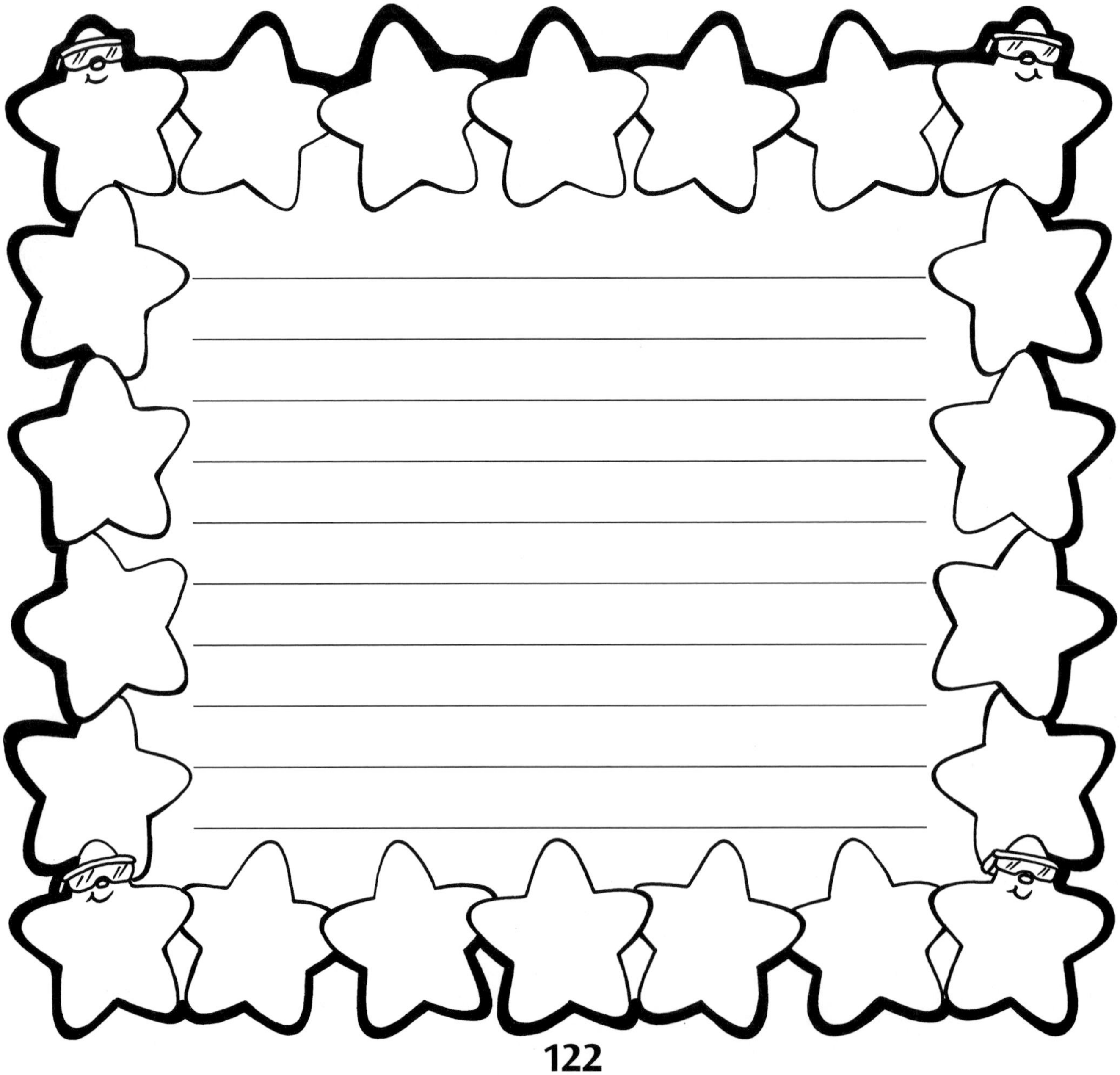

© Carson-Dellosa ✻ CD-104163 ✻ Scrapbooking Student Writing

The question for my science fair project was, "Which type of light allows pea plants to grow the tallest?" I tested fluorescent light, sunlight, and regular lightbulbs. The pea plants that grew in sunlight grew the tallest. They were about 18 inches tall! I really liked doing my project and getting to check the results every day. It's fun to learn about science and guess what is going to happen in an experiment.

Directions for Assembly:

1. Instruct students to color the clip art (page 125 or 126). If they prefer, they can write their titles on white paper instead of using the clip art titles.

2. Have students cut out all of the art.

3. Tell them to carefully glue their titles onto the mat paper (optional). They may need to cut the mat paper to fit their titles.

4. Ask students to arrange the pieces on their background paper before they start gluing. When everything is ready, let them carefully glue the pieces in place.

Teacher Tips:

1. Students can complete this page even if they did not enter the science fair. After a visit to the science fair, they can write about the projects they thought were the most interesting.

2. If you choose Writing Option 2 and students need additional room, provide lined paper and let them attach it to the backs of their scrapbook pages. Or, students can each use an additional piece of background paper and create a second page for their scrapbooks. Each student can mat the writing on a different color piece of paper to add interest.

Science Fair

Each Student Needs:

- 1 piece of background paper
- 1 copy of clip art (page 125 or 126, not both)
- ½ page of paper to mat title (optional)
- pencil
- markers or colorful pencils
- scissors
- glue or glue stick
- any additional embellishments you wish to provide

Writing Assignment:

Option 1: Distribute copies of page 125. Have students write brief descriptions of the most interesting projects they saw at the science fair. If a student entered the science fair, she can write about the details of her own project, as well. Students can also use this page to highlight the sensory experiences of attending the science fair. Have each student write detailed descriptions of the sights, smells, sounds, or textures that she observed.

Option 2: Distribute copies of page 126. Have each student use the large template to write a description of the science fair experience. What was it like? If he entered, how did he do? Did he enjoy making his project? Was it hard? What was the topic? If he did not enter, what did he see? What was the most interesting project he saw, and why does he think so?

One time, I felt lucky when a magician picked me to be her assistant on stage during a performance at our school.

I feel lucky to have a best friend like Erin. She always does fun things and cheers me up if I'm sad.

Lucky Me!

I feel lucky to have two funny kittens that jump in my lap and purr when I get home from school.

I feel lucky to have my grandmother living with us because she plays games with me and reads me stories.

Directions for Assembly:

1. Instruct students to color the clip art (page 129 or 130). If they prefer, they can write their titles on white paper instead of using the clip art titles.

2. Have students cut out all of the art.

3. Tell them to carefully glue their titles onto the mat paper (optional). They may need to cut the mat paper to fit their titles.

4. Ask students to arrange the pieces on their background paper before they start gluing. When everything is ready, let them carefully glue the pieces in place.

Teacher Tip:

Assign each student a lucky charm. Have students research the history of how each item came to be known as "lucky." Let students present their findings to the class or write about it using the template on page 130. If you choose this option or Writing Option 2 and students need additional room, provide lined paper and let them attach it to the backs of their scrapbook pages. Or, students can each use an additional piece of background paper and create a second page for their scrapbooks. Each student can mat the writing on a different color piece of paper to add interest.

St. Patrick's Day

Each Student Needs:

- 1 piece of background paper
- 1 copy of clip art (page 129 or 130, not both)
- ½ page of paper to mat title (optional)
- pencil
- markers or colorful pencils
- scissors
- glue or glue stick
- any additional embellishments you wish to provide

Writing Assignment:

Option 1: Distribute copies of page 129. Have each student write brief descriptions of people and things in her life that she feels lucky to have. For example, she might write that she is lucky to have her family, her dog, her own room, or her favorite toy. Each student can also write about times in her life when she felt lucky, like the time she won a raffle, found a dollar on the ground, or got a special part in a play.

Option 2: Distribute copies of page 130. Have each student use the large template to write a description of a time when he felt especially lucky. Perhaps he even has a lucky charm that he believes contributed to his good luck. Or, you can reverse the assignment and ask each student to write about an unlucky experience when nothing seemed to be going his way.

128

Lucky Me!

Lucky Me!

"Toad-ally" Awesome!

I wish I could have flown with a jet pack over Pluto for spring break. I want a red jet pack that goes really fast so that I can fly around all of the time. I would even use it to get to school in the morning instead of riding the bus. If I had a jet pack, I would go into outer space every day. If I could have flown to Pluto for spring break, I would have seen how big it really is. I bet Pluto isn't as small as it looks on the poster in Mrs. Anderson's classroom, but I bet it is definitely smaller than Earth. Mrs. Anderson says Pluto is really cold, so I would need to wear an extra thick coat for the trip! I wonder if I would meet any aliens while I was there?

Directions for Assembly:

1. Instruct students to color the clip art (page 133 or 134). If they prefer, they can write their titles on white paper instead of using the clip art titles.

2. Have students cut out all of the art.

3. Tell them to carefully glue their titles onto the mat paper (optional). They may need to cut the mat paper to fit their titles.

4. Ask students to arrange the pieces on their background paper before they start gluing. When everything is ready, let them carefully glue the pieces in place.

Teacher Tips:

1. If you choose Writing Option 2, remind students to be extremely descriptive. The more adjectives and descriptive dialogue they include, the more they will draw their audience into their "toad-ally" awesome ideal spring breaks.

2. If you choose Writing Option 2 and students need additional room, provide lined paper and let them attach it to the backs of their scrapbook pages. Or, students can each use an additional piece of background paper and create a second page for their scrapbooks. Each student can mat the writing on a different color piece of paper to add interest.

Spring Break

Each Student Needs:

- 1 piece of background paper
- 1 copy of clip art (page 133 or 134, not both)
- ½ page of paper to mat title (optional)
- pencil
- markers or colorful pencils
- scissors
- glue or glue stick
- any additional embellishments you wish to provide

Writing Assignment:

Option 1: Distribute copies of page 133. Have students think of some of the highlights of spring break. Have each student write two or three sentences about each of her favorite moments or events on a frog or lily pad template. Remind students to include funny stories or important moments that made spring break "toad-ally" awesome!

Option 2: Distribute copies of page 134. Instead of writing about what they did during spring break, have students write about what they did not do. Have students brainstorm about things they wish they could have done during the break. Ideas can be as realistic or fantastic as they wish—trips to Mars, guest appearances in new movies, shopping sprees with famous musicians, playing first base for a favorite professional baseball team, etc.

132

"Toad-ally" Awesome!

Spring

Break Was

Spring Break Was

"Toad-ally" Awesome!

Going Places

Yellowstone National Park

Last summer my family visited three national parks. They were Yellowstone, Zion, and Yosemite. All three of the parks were so beautiful! My two sisters really liked Zion National Park the best, but Yosemite National Park was my favorite of all of the places we visited.

Zion National Park

Yosemite National Park

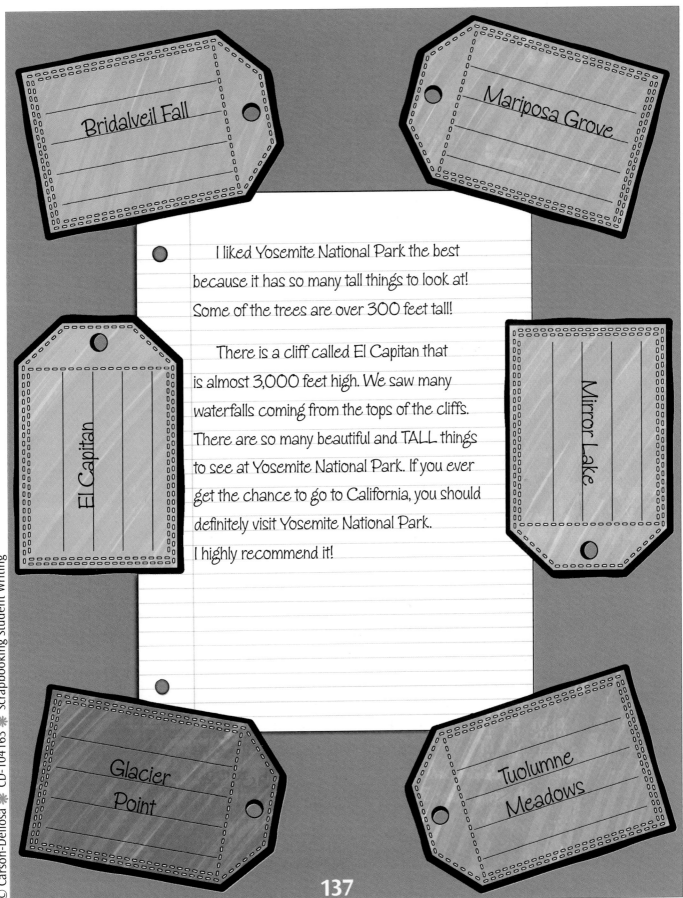

Bridalveil Fall

Mariposa Grove

El Capitan

Mirror Lake

I liked Yosemite National Park the best because it has so many tall things to look at! Some of the trees are over 300 feet tall!

There is a cliff called El Capitan that is almost 3,000 feet high. We saw many waterfalls coming from the tops of the cliffs. There are so many beautiful and TALL things to see at Yosemite National Park. If you ever get the chance to go to California, you should definitely visit Yosemite National Park. I highly recommend it!

Glacier Point

Tuolumne Meadows

Directions for Assembly:

1. Instruct students to color the clip art (pages 139–140). If they prefer, they can write their titles on white paper instead of using the clip art titles.

2. Have students cut out all of the art.

3. Tell them to carefully glue their titles onto the mat paper (optional). They may need to cut the mat paper to fit their titles.

4. Ask students to arrange the pieces on their background paper before they start gluing. When everything is ready, let them carefully glue the pieces in place.

Teacher Tips:

1. Consider printing the copies of pages 139–140 on colorful paper so that students will not need to color the tags using markers or colorful pencils.

2. Before beginning this activity, make a list of all of the field trips that the class has taken during the year. Use your calendar to remember them all!

3. This page can be completed as a one-page project (see the cover of this book) or as a two-page project (see pages 136–137), depending on students' writing abilities. For a one-page project, have students write their descriptions on the camera templates. For a two-page project, have students start writing their descriptions on their camera templates and provide lined paper for them to continue their stories.

4. If lined paper is necessary, each student can mat the writing on a different color piece of paper to add interest.

Field Trips

Each Student Needs:

- 1 or 2 pieces of background paper
- 1 copy of clip art (page 139)
- 1 copy of clip art (page 140)
- ½ page of paper to mat title (optional)
- lined paper (optional)
- pencil
- markers or colorful pencils
- scissors
- glue or glue stick
- any additional embellishments you wish to provide

Writing Assignment:

Option 1: Distribute copies of pages 139–140. Instruct students to write the name of each place the class visited during the year on a separate tag. You can also have them write the date of each field trip on the tag. Then, have each student write about his favorite field trip on the camera template. Tell him to include why it was his favorite and details or anecdotes that made it a great field trip. If he needs additional space, provide lined paper for him to continue his writing.

Option 2: Instead of writing about field trips, have students write about family trips. On each tag, have students write the name of a place they have visited (or would like to visit) with their families. Trip locations can be real or imaginary! Then, have students write all of the details about their favorite trips on their camera templates. If students need additional space, provide lined paper for them to continue their writing.

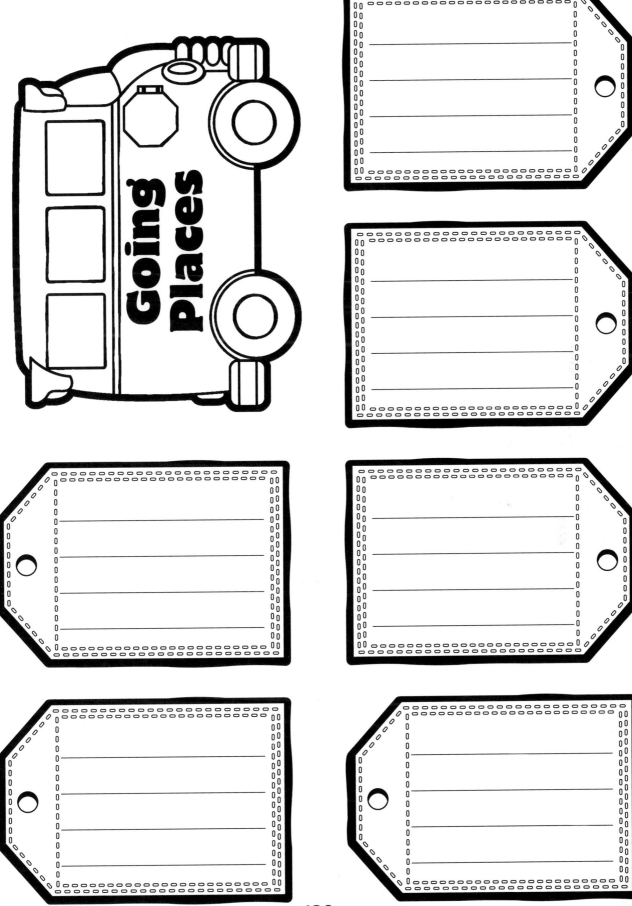

Going Places

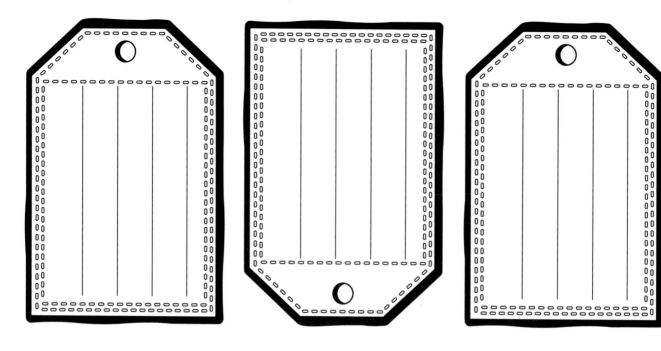

140

My Favorite Books

Gooney Bird Greene

The Mystery of the Stolen Statue

Owen Foote, Mighty Scientist

Jumanji

Amber Brown Is Not a Crayon

Freckle Juice

Tornado

Ruby Lu, Brave and True

Judy Moody

How to Be Cool in the Third Grade

Little House in the Big Woods

A Chair for My Mother

Guys from Space

The Boxcar Children

Directions for Assembly:

1. Instruct students to color the clip art (page 143 or 144). If they prefer, they can write their titles on white paper instead of using the clip art titles.

2. Have students cut out all of the art.

3. Tell them to carefully glue their titles onto the mat paper (optional). They may need to cut the mat paper to fit their titles.

4. Ask students to arrange the pieces on their background paper before they start gluing. When everything is ready, let them carefully glue the pieces in place.

Teacher Tips:

1. Consider printing the copies of page 143 on colorful paper so that students will not need to color the bookshelf using markers or colorful pencils.

2. Have more advanced writers write summaries of their favorite books on lined paper. Or, each student can write a new ending for her favorite book, write dialogue as if she were her favorite character, create a new chapter for the book, etc. Each student should cut out her completed writing and glue it to the bookshelf template (page 143).

3. If you choose Writing Option 2, consider matting the writing on a different color piece of paper to add interest.

Favorite Books

Each Student Needs:

- 1 piece of background paper
- 1 copy of clip art (page 143 or 144, not both)
- ½ page of paper to mat title (optional)
- lined paper (if using Writing Option 2)
- pencil
- markers or colorful pencils
- scissors
- glue or glue stick
- any additional embellishments you wish to provide

Writing Assignment:

Option 1: Distribute copies of page 143. Have each student brainstorm a list of her favorite books. Tell students to write the titles of their favorite books on the book spine templates. They can trace the spine templates onto colorful paper so that they will have enough spines to fill their bookshelves (or provide copies of page 144). Have students glue the spines onto their bookshelves.

Option 2: Distribute copies of page 144. Have each student think of his favorite literary character. On the writing templates, have him write the book title, author, and a brief description of his favorite character. Then, on the book spines, have him write words that describe the character's personality. Finally, have each student write a letter on lined paper to the character as if they were pen pals. Or, have him write the letter as if he were the character writing to a pen pal.

142

© Carson-Dellosa ✳ CD-104163 ✳ Scrapbooking Student Writing

My Favorite Books

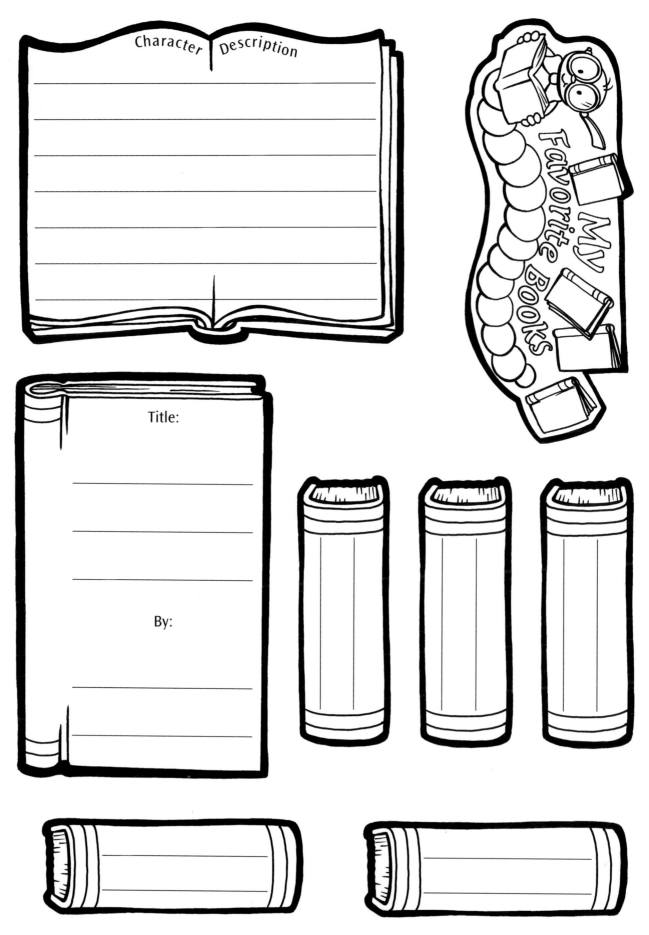

Character | Description

Title:

By:

LET'S GET MOVING!

I like basketball because my brother taught me to play when I was eight years old. I practice a lot. I hope I can learn to make a three-point shot someday!

I'm going to start playing ice hockey when I'm in the sixth grade. I already know how to ice skate, but I can't join a team until next year. I can't wait!

Soccer is my favorite sport because it is fun to watch and really fun to play. Soccer is hard, though. You have to work hard to be a good player, but it is worth it!

My sister is a competitive ice skater. Sometimes, I go skating during her lessons. She is a really good skater. She has even won three medals.

146

I started taking tennis lessons last summer. I'm not very good yet, but I really like it. My mom practices with me. Maybe someday, I'll be good enough to turn pro!

My big brother plays baseball. He is a catcher. He says when I get a little older he will teach me how to throw the ball really far like he does.

Football is a fun sport because you have to learn a lot of plays. I really like to play quarterback and try to throw long passes. My friends and I play football during recess whenever we can.

My sister takes ballet lessons. She really enjoys it, especially when she gets to dance on her toes. It's really cool, but it looks like it hurts!

Directions for Assembly:

1. Instruct students to color the clip art (pages 149–150). If they prefer, they can write their titles on white paper instead of using the clip art titles.

2. Have students cut out all of the art.

3. Tell them to carefully glue their titles onto the mat paper (optional). They may need to cut the mat paper to fit their titles.

4. Ask students to arrange the pieces on their background paper before they start gluing. When everything is ready, let them carefully glue the pieces in place.

Teacher Tips:

1. This page can be completed as a one-page project or as a two-page project, depending on students' writing abilities and interests. For a one-page project, have students fill in the templates for their four favorite activities. For a two-page project, have students fill in 6–8 of the templates.

2. Have advanced writers use Writing Option 2 for a different two-page project. Tell students to write paragraphs on lined paper about all of the activity templates they fill in. They should have room for 4–6 paragraphs in addition to the activity templates on two scrapbook pages.

3. If you choose Writing Option 2, let students mat their writing on different color pieces of paper to add interest.

Sports & Fitness

Each Student Needs:

- 2 pieces of background paper
- 1 copy of clip art (page 149)
- 1 copy of clip art (page 150)
- ½ page of paper to mat title (optional)
- lined paper (if using Writing Option 2)
- pencil
- markers or colorful pencils
- scissors
- glue or glue stick
- any additional embellishments you wish to provide

Writing Assignment:

Option 1: Instruct students to fill in at least four of the activity templates on pages 149–150 by writing about some of their favorite activities. If their favorite activities aren't illustrated, tell them to fill in the question mark box with sentences about those activities. Remind them to use complete sentences. Also, if there is room on each template, have each student write a second sentence that tells why the activity is one of his favorites.

Option 2: Instruct students to fill in the activity templates as described above. Then, tell them to choose two or three of their favorites. Have students write paragraphs on lined paper that describe why these are their favorite activities. Or, ask students to focus on one favorite activity and describe their goals; maybe a student wants to score several times in one game, be an Olympic champion, or be a collegiate or professional athlete someday.

© Carson-Dellosa ✳ CD-104163 ✳ Scrapbooking Student Writing

LET'S GET MOVING!

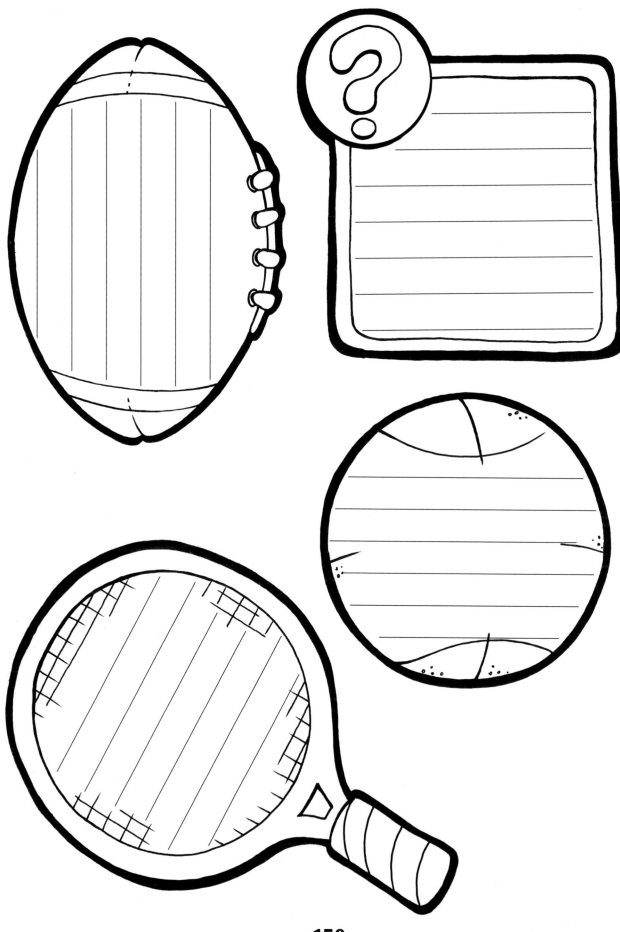

Directions for Assembly:

1. Instruct students to color the clip art (page 153 or 154). If they prefer, they can write their titles on white paper instead of using the clip art titles.

2. Have students cut out all of the art.

3. Tell them to carefully glue their titles onto the mat paper (optional). They may need to cut the mat paper to fit their titles.

4. Ask students to arrange the pieces on their background paper before they start gluing. When everything is ready, let them carefully glue the pieces in place.

Teacher Tips:

1. Remind students that they can be accomplished without receiving actual awards. Sometimes, they might receive awards for their achievements; other times, they will receive only praise. Still other times, they might feel like they've achieved great things without receiving any form of recognition from other people.

2. If you choose Writing Option 2 and students need additional room, provide lined paper and let them attach it to the backs of their scrapbook pages. Or, students can each use an additional piece of background paper and create a second page for their scrapbooks. Each student can mat the writing on a different color piece of paper to add interest.

Honors & Achievements

Each Student Needs:

- 1 piece of background paper
- 1 copy of clip art (page 153 or 154, not both)
- ½ page of paper to mat title (optional)
- pencil
- markers or colorful pencils
- scissors
- glue or glue stick
- any additional embellishments you wish to provide

Writing Assignment:

Option 1: Distribute copies of page 153. Tell students to think of academic achievements that make them proud. These achievements do not necessarily need to be grades or certificates that they have received; students could be proud of reading long chapter books, learning new math concepts, or doing good work on science fair projects. Tell students to write one achievement in a complete sentence on each award ribbon template.

Option 2: Distribute copies of page 154. Have each student fill in the diploma by writing about his proudest academic achievement. Tell him to describe the success and write about why it is so special to him. Was it difficult to achieve? How did he feel when he reached the goal? Why is it his proudest achievement?

© Carson-Dellosa ✳ CD-104163 ✳ Scrapbooking Student Writing

Achievements

_____ **has achieved** _____
(Your Name)

_____

This is a special achievement because _____

_____

_____

_____

_____

_____

_____

_____

_____

_____

_____

© Carson-Dellosa ✹ CD-104163 ✹ Scrapbooking Student Writing

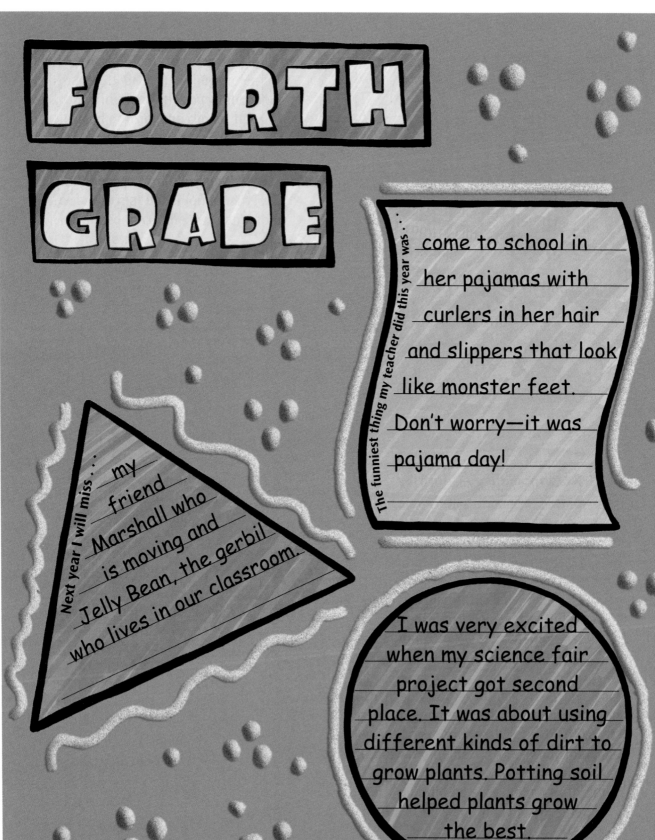

FOURTH GRADE

The funniest thing my teacher did this year was . . . come to school in her pajamas with curlers in her hair and slippers that look like monster feet. Don't worry—it was pajama day!

Next year I will miss . . . my friend Marshall who is moving and Jelly Bean, the gerbil who lives in our classroom.

I was very excited when my science fair project got second place. It was about using different kinds of dirt to grow plants. Potting soil helped plants grow the best.

WAS

COOL!

My friend Kumiko drew pictures of all of us for presents. She is a great artist. She gave us our drawings last week during recess. Mine looks just like me!

The most surprising thing about this year was . . . when Mrs. Jenkins, the principal, told us that the President was going to visit our school! We got to hear him speak in the auditorium about learning to read.

The best project we did this year was . . . decorate our classroom doors to look like our favorite books. We chose *Tales of a Fourth Grade Nothing.*

✳ CD-104163 ✳ Scrapbooking Student Writing

157

Directions for Assembly:

1. Instruct students to color the clip art (pages 159–160). If they prefer, they can write their titles on white paper instead of using the clip art titles.

2. Have students cut out all of the art.

3. Tell them to carefully glue their titles onto the mat paper (optional). They may need to cut the mat paper to fit their titles.

4. Ask students to arrange the pieces on their background paper before they start gluing. When everything is ready, let them carefully glue the pieces in place.

Teacher Tips:

1. Consider printing the copies of pages 159–160 on colorful paper so that students will not need to color the shapes using markers or colorful pencils.

2. Brainstorm a list of prompts for the blank shapes so that you will have a list ready in case students have trouble thinking of topics.

3. If you choose Writing Option 2, let students mat their writing on different color pieces of paper to add interest.

4. For advanced writers, consider using Writing Option 2 and have students write paragraphs about all of the templates they fill in. They should have room for 4–6 paragraphs in addition to the templates on two scrapbook pages.

End of the Year

Each Student Needs:

- 2 pieces of background paper
- 1 copy of clip art (page 159)
- 1 copy of clip art (page 160)
- ½ page of paper to mat title (optional)
- lined paper (if using Writing Option 2)
- pencil
- markers or colorful pencils
- scissors
- glue or glue stick
- any additional embellishments you wish to provide

Writing Assignment:

Option 1: Instruct students to fill in the shapes on pages 159–160 by writing sentences about some of the best things that happened during the school year. Tell them to fill in the blank shapes with sentences about other great things that are not already listed. Remind them to use complete sentences. Also, if there is room on the shapes, have each student write a second sentence that explains why she chose to highlight each item or event.

Option 2: Instruct students to fill in the shapes as described above. Then, tell them to choose two or three of their favorite topics. Have them write paragraphs on lined paper that describe these favorite items or events. Is there a funny or interesting story about the particular memory? Remind students to be descriptive and use good adjectives.

COOL!

The best project we did this year was . . .

Next year I will miss . . .

GRADE

THIRD

WAS

FIFTH

FOURTH

The funniest thing my teacher did this year was . . .

_____
_____
_____
_____
_____
_____
_____
_____
_____

_____
_____
_____
_____
_____
_____

The most surprising thing about this year was . . .

_____
_____
_____
_____
_____
_____
_____
_____
_____

_____
_____
_____
_____
_____
_____
_____
_____